## Macmillan Computer Science Series

*Consulting Editor*:
Professor F. H. Sumner, University of Manchester

*continued overleaf*

# A
# Book on
# C

## Third Edition

**B. A. E. Meekings**
**T. P. Kudrycki**
and
**M. D. Soren**

MACMILLAN

First edition 1984
Reprinted 1985, 1986
Second edition 1988
Reprinted 1990
Third edition 1993

Published by
THE MACMILLAN PRESS LTD
Houndmills, Basingstoke, Hampshire RG21 2XS
and London
Companies and representatives
throughout the world

ISBN 0–333–56919–9

A catalogue record for this book is available
from the British Library.

Printed in Hong Kong

For
Marion, Judy and Paul,
Toby, Tim, Lucy, and Ben,
Denver,
Kasia

# Contents

# Preface

When we wrote the first edition of this book, it was with the intention of providing an introduction to a powerful and complex programming language. As C gained in popularity, it became apparent that a simple introduction was not enough, and the second edition included a number of topics which we had originally regarded as "advanced". The third edition is expanded yet again, and now covers the new ANSI standard C.

Although the C standard was the principal reason for the third edition, we have made other changes - for example, the style analysis suite has been rewritten entirely in C, rather than using a variety of UNIX system tools; and we are now able to offer the text of all the examples, plus the style program and a mini-compiler, in machine-readable form on a floppy diskette.

We believe that we have a unique approach to the teaching of a programming language, with emphasis on programming style and a structured methodology, as well as on details of the language itself.

C appears set to be the "language of choice" for many professional and recreational programmers for at least the rest of the decade. We hope that learning it gives the same lift to your programming experience as it has done to ours.

September 1992

Tom Kudrycki

Brian Meekings

Michael Soren

# Introduction

Programming is communication. In attempting to teach a programming language we are trying to provide the learner with a means of communication, a means of expressing himself or herself. At first sight it will appear that the communication will be one way, between the program writer and the machine on which his or her program is processed. This view is too simplistic, for the communication occurs on a number of different levels.

Certainly it is important that the programmer is sufficiently familiar with the language selected to write the program to produce concise and efficient code, but it should not be forgotten that, after successful development, a program will need to communicate with its user while executing. This aspect of communication is now, justifiably, receiving considerable attention. It is no longer satisfactory that the program produces the correct result - it should also be easy to use and should be 'bulletproof', which is to say that, no matter how inaccurate the user's input, the program should always provide a sensible and intelligible response. In the jargon, the program should be 'user friendly'. An argument can be made that a big share of the ever-increasing software development cost can be attributed to the market's need for better and more eloquent user interfaces. Elaborate and intuitive graphical interfaces are becoming more and more common in even simple software products.

A further level of communication, all too frequently neglected, is that between program writer and program reader. Program writers frequently assume that the only readers of the program will be themselves and a computer. The consequence of this assumption is that the program may be tedious and difficult to assimilate by anyone given the task of modifying, or simply reading, the original. Like everything else of man's creation, software will not be perfect, and should be written with the knowledge that it will need to be maintained. This means taking all reasonable steps to ensure that the program logic is lucidly expressed by the text, and the layout and presentation of a program help considerably in this. Unfortunately, there are constraints imposed by some language implementations that inhibit good presentation. Thus when using a BASIC interpreter with access to a limited amount of memory, there will be pressure on a programmer to omit comments and to discard unnecessary spaces. We recognise the pressures, but regret their effect on the intelligibility of programs.

The concept of program style encompasses the presentation, layout and readability of computer programs. These principles apply to any programming

1

language, whether high level or low level. The factors that contribute to program style are undoubtedly highly subjective, and thus contentious. Our contribution to the debate is to enumerate what we consider to constitute a reasonable set of metrics, whose application can be automated, and to associate with each of the program examples within the text a 'style score'. At the foot of every nontrivial program you will see this style score enclosed in square brackets. For small examples the style score can be sensitive to small changes in presentation, for example, the addition of a blank line. Nonetheless, we give it so that the reader can judge its usefulness. A small C program is illustrated in example I.1 to give a hint of what is to follow. The derivation of the style score is detailed in Appendix 1. Suffice it to say here that the score is a percentage, and that the higher the score, the more 'elegant' the program.

The programming language C is a powerful language, and deserves its high and still increasing popularity as one of the most important programming languages currently available. Without wishing to over-stress program style and the importance of good program design, we feel that it is necessary to point out that no programming language is, as yet, so powerful as to conceal flaws in program logic or to make its clear exposition unnecessary. Sound program logic is achieved by design, and in recent years considerable attention has been given to program design methods. Whether a structured program is achieved after the design stage will depend on the person or persons who translate the design into a program in an appropriate programming language - a not inconsiderable task. The book by Dahl *et al.* (1972) is worthy of the reader's attention (see References).

Programs can become such complex artefacts that a new art and science of software engineering came into existence in recent years. We can truly speak of software being engineered, an activity which may involve many tens or hundreds of people and which requires coordination and control over many of its aspects. With this in mind, it is not surprising to find software tools produced to assist in this engineering. The software tools philosophy espoused by Kernighan and Plauger (1976) and realised in UNIX is an impressive demonstration of the importance of this approach. We believe that UNIX and C have significantly expanded our own computing horizons, and thoroughly recommend the experience to others.

*Example I.1*

```
#include <stdio.h>
#include <string.h>

/* to resort the letters of a word into alphabetical
   order - e.g. the basis of an anagram dictionary */

int
main ()
{
```

```
char word[21], min;
int i, j, pos, len;

printf ("Gimme a word...");
scanf ("%s", word);

len = strlen(word);
for (i=0; i<len; i++) {
    min = '~';      /* the last character */
    pos = 0;
    for (j = 0; j < len; j++)
        if (word[j] < min) {
            min = word[j];
            pos = j;
        } /* found a smaller letter */

    printf ("%c", min);
    word[pos] = '~';
}

printf ("\n");

return 0;
} /* main */

[ style 67.7 ]
```

There are a number of texts that describe the UNIX system and C. That by Bourne (1982) we found particularly useful. Kernighan and Ritchie's (1978) book remains the definitive reference for the original version of C, while the experienced user might better himself by reading Feuer (1982).

Different flavours of C have evolved over the years. Many of the features of the language are common to all its implementations. There are, however, many implementations which lack capabilities found in others. On the other hand, many C implementations provide language extensions specific to a particular computer manufacturer or operating system. In an effort to standardise the C language implementation, the American National Standards Institute (ANSI) has formed a committee to define a version of the language attempting to fulfil a very difficult task of being standard across a wide variety of machines and operating systems. A document describing the standard was completed in December 1989 and published in 1990. The second edition of Kernighan and Ritchie's book (1988) has been expanded to include the ANSI standard.

In this book, the language C as defined by ANSI standard X3.159-1989 is described. All C implementations conforming to the standard are referred to as conformant and the programs written strictly in accordance with the rules defined in the standard as portable, on the understanding that more and more C compilers are conforming to the standard, and therefore the programs written in standard C are becoming more widely portable. Whenever feasible, we attempt to point out differences between the standard and the earlier C implementations, with emphasis on points to which a prudent C developer should pay particular attention. We also offer some advice on making your nonstandard programs as widely portable as possible and prepare for availability of an ANSI C compiler on your installation.

The first chapter of this book describes the structure of C programs. Chapter 2 introduces functions, contrasting them with macros. Chapter 3 deals with input and output, emphasising the importance of the interface between the program and its environment.

Chapters 4 and 5 explain the two features of any programming language that give it its power - the control constructs of conditional branching and looping. Operators are introduced in chapter 6, while chapter 7 illustrates the use of arrays and strings.

This is the point at which all the 'basic' features of C have been covered. The remaining chapters describe what we consider to be 'advanced' features - derived data types in chapter 8, data structures in chapter 9 and the C pre-processor in chapter 10. Chapter 11 presents some guidance on program style, which we could define loosely as that enigmatic quality that distinguishes adequate programs from superlative ones. Finally, chapter 12 lists the functions and features provided by conformant C implementations, stressing the portability issues and offering guidance in providing some of the standard C functionality on your local implementation.

In learning any programming language we have found that examples which, as well as illustrating language features, stimulate the reader's interest, are of particular importance. We have tried to present an interesting variety of examples.

In order to make the learning process easier and more enjoyable, and to save you a lot of typing should you find our programs interesting, we can provide on MS-DOS 360K diskettes all the substantial examples reproduced in this book, and the style analysis program used for our style scoring throughout the book. In addition, we include the source code for a rather larger programming example - a C program, which we call RatC, that accepts as input a program written in a subset of C and produces as output an intermediate code version of the program. This intermediate version can then be given to RatC to preprocess and produce an assembly code for a variety of machines. RatC can in this way even reproduce itself. We provide the user with sufficient information to implement his own small C compiler. To order the diskettes, write to:

Soren Associates
PO Box 7403
Somerset
NJ 08875-7403
USA

and enclose a cheque for $25, drawn on a US bank.

Above all, C is a language to enjoy. The kind of thing you always wanted to be able to do in other programming languages becomes possible in C - but be warned that its power, as well as getting you out of trouble quickly, can get you into trouble just as quickly.

# 1 Program Structure

In the introduction we attempted to show that programming must be undertaken in a disciplined and organised manner. If the resulting program is to display the benefit of this approach then the programmer must be thoroughly familiar with the program structure dictated by the programming language that he, or she, is to use.

## FUNCTIONS

A C program consists of one or more functions. One of these functions must have the name *main*. A program is executed when the underlying operating system causes control to be passed to the function *main* of the user's program. The function *main* differs from the other functions in a program in that it *must* be defined, in order to provide a starting point for execution, and its parameters, if they exist, are provided by the operating system. It is usual, but not essential, for *main* to be the first function of the program text.

Viewed simply, a function name is nothing more than a collective name for a group of declarations and statements enclosed in curly brackets or braces {}. The function *useless* below is of little value since it contains no executable statements. Its only purpose is to illustrate the appearance of a minimal function.

```
useless ()
{
}
```

The parentheses following the function name are essential, and will later be shown to be more useful than the present example suggests.

If we assume that *main* is the first function defined in a C program text then, because no function may contain the definition of another function, the definitions of the subsidiary functions of the program text will follow. There may be only two or three such functions, in which case their purposes will be easy to determine, or there may be many. There is no special ordering of the functions dictated by the programming language C (in contrast to Pascal which, despite advocating the structured approach to problem solving, precludes its effective use by insisting that all functions be defined before they are used). However, after emphasising the value of a program as a means of communication, it would be foolish to suggest that an arbitrary order for the functions would be as good as an order with some rationale. The function definitions could be arranged in alphabetical order, or they could be grouped according to their purpose. This latter ordering is not so easy to achieve but can frequently be more helpful.

## IDENTIFIERS

An identifier in C, whether it represents a function name or a variable, consists of any sequence of the characters [a-z, A-Z, 0-9,_]. The first character of an identifier must not be a digit. Upper and lower case letters are distinct, so that, for example, the identifiers *count*, *Count* and *COUNT* represent three different quantities. Internal identifiers in strictly portable programs should not be longer than 31 characters. In some older, non-conformant compilers, only the first eight characters are significant.

Identifiers are characterised by the two attributes 'type' and 'storage class'. It is also possible to modify the behaviour of identifiers by specifying the 'type qualifier'. The type of an identifier determines the type of object that it will be used to represent; so, for example, *int*, *float* and *char* qualify an identifier as representing an integer, a real (or floating point) number and a single character respectively. The full list of available types is given in appendix 2. An identifier's storage class determines its 'scope' - the way in which it can be accessed from other parts of the program.

## FILES AND THE STORAGE CLASS *external*

For programmer convenience, a large program may have its text spread over several files. To illustrate the effect of file structure on C programs and the symbols or names used within them, consider the examples given below, in which items within the same file are enclosed by a box.

*Example 1.1*

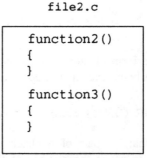

```
        file1.c                    file2.c

    main()                     function2()
    {                          {
    }                          }
    function1()                function3()
    {                          {
    }                          }
```

In example 1.1, if we ignore *main*, any of the three functions could legitimately contain references to each of the remaining two. *main* may call any of the other three functions. This is possible because all function names belong to the storage class *external*. Any symbol name from this storage class may be referenced across files.

A function may also contain a call of itself. This is known as a recursive call, and an example of such a call will be found in the function *drawtree* given as part of an example in chapter 9.

## STORAGE CLASS *automatic*

In order that the functions we define can perform some useful role they will need to manipulate data. As in most programming languages the name and type of every data item must be declared. A declaration does not necessarily reserve storage to be associated with the identifier, but rather establishes the type and storage class of the declared identifier. In the example below *size* is declared to be an integer and its storage class is *automatic*.

```
main( )
{
     int size;
}
```

The identifier *size* is local to the function *main* and may only be used within *main*. If the name *size* is used in any other function in the program it is not then connected in any way with the data item of the same name in the function *main*. The storage class is known as *automatic* because, for any identifier in the class, storage space is allocated when the function is entered and given up when exit is made from the function. In standard C, the automatic storage class can be explicitly specified in a declaration by using keyword *auto*. Such specification is, however, redundant since *automatic* is the default storage class for any identifier declared within a function.

```
main( )
{
     auto int size;
}
```

While this form of storage is economical, in that it is needed only when a function is being executed, it does not meet all our requirements.

## STORAGE CLASS *static*

Imagine that, as part of a check upon the operation of a program, it is necessary to count the number of times that a function was executed. The count should be local or private to the function but the associated storage should be preserved from one call of the function to the next in order that the count may be accumulated. An identifier with storage class *automatic* is clearly inappropriate, since its value would be lost between successive calls of the function. Consider example 1.2: the identifier *count* has been defined as type integer with storage class *static*. It could be used to accumulate the number of calls of *function1*, because the value of static variables is retained across invocations.

*Example 1.2*

file1.c

```
main()
{
}

function1()
{
    static int count;
}
```

file2.c

```
function2()
{
}

function3()
{
}
```

As another example, suppose that two or more functions are used to manipulate the contents of a table. Each function will require access to the table and its associated pointers. It might also be desirable to protect the table from corruption by ensuring that no other function of the program gains access to the table. Both requirements can be met by using data items belonging to the *static* storage class within the same file.

*Example 1.3*

file1.c

```
main()
{
    int size;
}
function1()
{
    int i:
}
```

file2.c

```
static int ptr;
function2()
{

}
function3()
{
    int i:
}
```

In example 1.3, the identifier *size* can only be used in *main*. The identifier *i* of *function1* has no logical connection with the identifier *i* of *function3*. The second file contains the definition of *ptr*. Both *function2* and *function3* may use the identifier *ptr*, as may any other function defined in that file. The storage class of *ptr* is not *automatic* but *static*. Identifier *ptr* is not accessible to a function in any other file. Note that it is not only function names that belong to the storage class *external*. We can declare the names of other data items so that they belong to this class. These names too may be referenced across files. If we change file1 of our example by adding the line

```
    extern int ptr;
```

and remove the word *static* from file2, as shown in example 1.4, then the function *main* can now reference the item *ptr* defined in file2.

*Example 1.4*

file1.c

```
main()
{
    extern int ptr;
    int size;
}
function1()
{
    int i;
}
```

file2.c

```
int ptr;
function2()
{

}
function3()
{
    int i;
}
```

If, however, the *extern* statement were to appear as the first line in file1 then all functions in that file could refer to *ptr*, and this would be the same object declared in file2. In distributing a program text across files in this fashion we would need to ensure that for each identifier name in the external storage class, other than function names, there was one declaration of this name that did not include the word *extern*. This is called the definition of the identifier. The prefix *static* must be omitted in this definition.


**STORAGE CLASS** *register*

This new storage class introduced by the ANSI standard implies that it is desirable to have the fastest possible access to the object thus defined. It may be possible to assign the object to one of the CPU registers and never allocate storage for it in the computer's main memory. Effectiveness of such requests is, however, implementation-defined and is not guaranteed by the standard. In the example below, it is suggested that function *main* makes frequent references to object *size* and desires the fastest possible access to it.

```
main()
{
    register int size;
}
```

## TYPE MODIFIERS

As the name implies, type modifiers alter some aspects of the object's behaviour. The *const* type modifier specifies that the object cannot be changed during program execution. The system can place such objects in a read-only-memory (ROM) or a protected memory segment. Objects so defined can be used to store values which are not modified by the program, such as physical or mathematical constants. The *volatile* type modifier is almost an opposite of *const*. It specifies that the object can be modified at any time by factors outside of the program, or that its modification can have other unknown side effects. Such objects are typically modified by hardware without any indication to the program. The system takes extra care in using the values of such objects. The two type modifiers are not mutually exclusive. Object *size* in the example below cannot be modified by the program, but it should be assumed that it is modifiable by the computer hardware.

```
main( )
{
    const volatile int size;
}
```

## THE C PREPROCESSOR

The preceding discussion on files assumes that it is sensible and convenient to divide a program text into multiple files and also that the names of the two or more files are passed to the C compiler for processing. There are circumstances, however, in which it might be convenient to divide our program physically between files but to treat it logically as a large program text in one file. This facility is made available by the C preprocessor.

Preprocessing is, as its name suggests, undertaken prior to compilation and provides two important facilities; the ability to 'include' files and the ability to 'define' text for macro replacement. These are extremely convenient facilities and, since frequent use is made of them, they are introduced at this early stage.

#### #include

Example 1.5 differs from example 1.1 in the addition of one line at the end of file1. This is sufficient to change the organisation of the program in a small but significant way. The 'include file' request must appear on a separate line and is treated as a request to replace the line itself by the contents of the file given, in this case file2.c. In some older compilers, all preprocessor requests must start at the left margin. Under the UNIX operating system, if the file name appears in double quote marks it is assumed to be in the current directory; if the file name is included instead in angle brackets, a special directory is assumed to be the location of the file. In either case the contents of the file replace the *include* directive and the combined text is passed on to the C compiler which treats it logically as one file of program text. Several files may be coalesced by use of suitable *include* directives. Included files may themselves contain *include* directives, but such nesting cannot exceed 8 levels in a strictly portable program. While this is a legitimate use of the included file facility, an included file more usually contains *define* directives. A file containing *define* directives is known as a header file and, by convention, has a filename ending in '.h'. Any file containing C program text has a name which ends with '.c'.

*Example 1.5*

```
        file1.c                         file2.c

  main()                          function2()
  {                               {
  }                               }
  function1()                     function3()
  {                               {
  }                               }
  #include "file2.c"
```

#### #define

The *define* directive provides the user with a macro replacement facility. The C preprocessor in this context is a macro processor, although this is not always appreciated by newcomers to this facility. The most common use of the *define* directive is of the form

```
#define DAYSINWEEK 7
```

The preprocessor will thereafter replace the text string 'DAYSINWEEK' throughout the entire text by the string '7'. In one sense this facility can be likened to the *const* type modifier or *const* section of a Pascal program in that it provides a means of removing all explicit constants from a program text and enables the user to use symbolic names instead. We think that it is good practice to gather all such definitions at the head of the program text file. It is even more desirable to use *const* type modifiers for that purpose, since objects defined through the normal type declarations will be checked for proper types during program compilation, whereas constants defined in *#define* directives are just character strings taken verbatim without any type checking. Before using *const* type modifiers instead of *#define* directives, one may consider, however, that many C compilers are still not strictly conformant and do not recognize type modifiers. In chapter 10, we will provide some suggestions for writing programs which can be compiled by both strictly conformant and older types of compilers.

The *define* directive is not restricted to use in the manner described above for program constants. It is, in general, much more powerful and useful, since it replaces one text string by another and will, as we shall see later, also deal with parameters.

## SIMPLE C CONSTRUCTS

In order that we may use examples to illustrate the points made in the text, we need, as has already become obvious, some programming language constructs. Even the simple examples need to demonstrate that they work by printing something. We therefore introduce the *printf* function.

```
printf ("The answer is 42");
```

*printf*, print formatted, is perhaps the most commonly used output function. Whatever text appears within the double quote marks is, with a few important exceptions, printed on the user's output device. Input and output statements became an integral part of the standard C language. Older versions of C did not define input and output statements but rather provided them within an implementation-defined commonly accessible library of such routines, which would be made available to the program via an *include* file. ANSI C sanctioned the use of such libraries and made them a part of the language definition, thus in principle making the standard library function names reserved. For example, use of

```
#include <stdio.h>
```

at the head of a program is a convenient way of obtaining access to some commonly used definitions. These definitions include several of the simpler input/output functions. We shall assume for convenience that the user is using

a visual display unit (VDU) to a multi-user or microcomputer system on which
C is available.

```
printf ("\nThe answer is 42\n");
```

This variant of the first *printf* statement prints a newline character, represented
by the character pair \n, before and after printing the string itself. All
statements in C are terminated by a semi-colon. There may be more than one
statement per line. An assignment statement is exemplified by

```
answer=42;   /* 42 is a decimal constant */
answer=052;  /* leading 0 means an octal constant */
answer=0x2a; /* leading 0x or 0X means a hex constant */
```

where we assume that *answer* has been declared to be an integer. Lastly, let us
note at this point that the braces {} may be used to enclose one or more C
statements

```
{ question=99; answer=42; }
```

The collective name for statements enclosed in this way is a compound
statement. It will become obvious from the examples that in C a comment is
any text string enclosed by /* and */.
    Further examples of the use of the *define* directive can now be given by
using the *printf* function. The definition

```
#define STARS printf("*********")
```

will cause the symbol *STARS* to be replaced by the call of the function *printf*.
When viewed in the context of the example given below it will be appreciated
that the *define* facility could save us some tedious typing.

```
#define STARS printf("*********")

main( )
{
    STARS;
    printf("\nThe answer is 42\n");
    STARS;
}
```

### *defining* VDU CHARACTERISTICS

We can use the *define* directive in another more useful way to improve the
quality, and thus the user friendliness, of the output produced by any program.
Most VDUs in common use have facilities to home the cursor, clear the screen,
and so on. Invariably to use these features means sending a special character
sequence to the terminal. The character sequence is not easy to remember

unless one uses it constantly; it varies from one manufacturer's product to another and frequently between different models from the same manufacturer. What we suggest is that these codes are set up once and for all using *define* directives. For a Lear Siegler ADM5 we would have

```
#define CLEAR    printf ("\033Y")
#define HOME     printf ("\036")
```

Recall that the backslash followed by n was used to denote a newline character. Backslash followed by a number can be used in *printf* and elsewhere in a C program, to denote the character defined by the ASCII code in octal which follows the backslash. A table of the ASCII characters with their octal representations is given in appendix 2. To clear the screen of this particular terminal we can send the escape character (ESC) followed by the letter Y. Since this clears from the cursor to the end of the screen, the HOME command should precede the CLEAR. This form of CLEAR command is given because ESC followed by a character sequence is a common way of expressing VDU directives.

The number of special features available on a VDU varies considerably. A VT100 terminal, for example, will offer cursor addressing, blinking, high-lighting, reverse video and other features all of which are selected by a special character sequence beginning with ESC. For any VDU these special features should be noted and appropriate *define* directives set up as illustrated in the examples. Thereafter all the *define* directives for one terminal should be collected together in a suitably named file. Any C program wishing to use these facilities need then only *include* this file at the head of the program and all the commands defined for that VDU become available.

## SUMMARY

In this chapter we have described the structure of C programs. We have illustrated the convenient and versatile mechanisms that are easily available to the programmer to help produce a well-organised and a well-structured program. We shall endeavour to reinforce these ideas through the examples that we present. Our presentation may not be perfect and may seem for the smaller examples to dominate the examples themselves. Effort spent on organisation, structure and layout of a program is worthwhile, and particularly useful for larger programs. If you find our examples easy to assimilate and find your way round, then use some of the same strategy on your programs. If on the other hand you feel the presentation or organisation could be improved, then learn from our failings and produce well-structured programs as a result.

# 2 Functions

As we have seen in the previous chapter, functions offer an easy way to construct a modular program. Since they are such an essential part of good C programming we shall introduce their facilities at an early stage to encourage familiarity with their use.

## SIMPLE FUNCTIONS

In order that our examples may achieve something, even if it is not especially useful, we will make use of the *printf* statement introduced earlier.

*Example 2.1*

```
#include "adm5.h"
#define  GAP printf("\n\n\n\n")

/* a program to print large letters */

main ()
{
    HOME; CLEAR;  GAP;          /* clear the screen */
    bigH ();      GAP;
    bigI ();      GAP;
}

/* bigH prints H as a 7*5 matrix of asterisks */

bigH ()
{
    printf ("*   *\n");
    printf ("*   *\n");
    printf ("*   *\n");
    printf ("*****\n");
    printf ("*   *\n");
    printf ("*   *\n");
    printf ("*   *\n");
}
```

```
/* bigI prints I as a 7*5 matrix of asterisks */

bigI ()
{
    printf ("*****\n");
    printf ("  *  \n");
    printf ("  *  \n");
    printf ("  *  \n");
    printf ("  *  \n");
    printf ("  *  \n");
    printf ("*****\n");
}
```

[ style 62.3 ]

Because the program does not do much, its structure, and the preprocessor facilities that it uses, are easily seen. The *include* file 'adm5.h' contains screen control instructions for a Lear Siegler ADM5.

In the body of the program, after clearing the screen, a call to the function *bigH* is made. When executed this function causes asterisks to be printed representing the character H in a 7 * 5 matrix of characters. Similarly *bigI* causes the character I to be printed. The symbol *GAP* ensures an appropriate separation between the characters and whatever follows them on the screen.

Anyone choosing to type example 2.1 into their own machine will quickly realise that they are typing identical *printf* statements several times over. Example 2.2 illustrates that by using the *define* facility of the preprocessor we can save writing and typing of text. Remember that the preprocessor will simply replace the defined symbol by its definition throughout the program text, and so the version of program 2.2 that reaches the compiler will be logically equivalent to program 2.1.

*Example 2.2*

```
#include "adm5.h"
#define  GAP printf("\n\n\n\n")

/* allstars prints all stars */
#define allstars printf ("*****\n")

/* endstars prints end stars */
#define endstars printf ("*   *\n")

/* midstar prints mid stars */
#define midstar printf ("  *  \n")

main ()
{
    HOME; CLEAR; GAP; /* clear the screen */
    bigH ();     GAP;
    bigI ();     GAP;
}
```

```
bigH ()
{
    endstars; endstars; endstars;
    allstars;
    endstars; endstars; endstars;
}

bigI ()
{
    allstars;
    midstar; midstar; midstar; midstar; midstar;
    allstars;
}

[ style 55.4 ]
```

Alternatively, the program can be rewritten using function calls instead of *defines* by declaring *allstars, endstars* and *midstar* as functions, as shown in example 2.3. The programs 2.2 and 2.3 are functionally, but not logically, equivalent, in the sense that, although the output from both is the same, in one case it is produced by a program with three functions, and in the other, by a program with six.

*Example 2.3*

```
#include "adm5.h"
#define  GAP printf("\n\n\n\n")

main ()
{
    HOME; CLEAR; GAP; /* clear the screen */
    bigH ();      GAP;
    bigI ();      GAP;
}

bigH ()
{
    endstars (); endstars (); endstars ();
    allstars ();
    endstars (); endstars (); endstars ();
}

bigI ()
{
    allstars ();
    midstar (); midstar (); midstar ();
    midstar (); midstar ();
    allstars ();
}

/* allstars(), endstars(), midstar() */
/* are now defined as functions      */
```

```
allstars ()
{ printf ("*****\n"); }

endstars ()
{ printf ("*    *\n"); }

midstar ()
{ printf ("  *  \n"); }

[ style 42.4 ]
```

## MACROS OR FUNCTIONS?

When executing, the program 2.3 produces the same results as the two previous versions of this program. Which is best depends on what criteria are used for the comparison. In example 2.2 the preprocessor replaces all symbols defined in a *define*. The transformed program is passed to the C compiler. When executed, the body of the function *bigH* causes seven *printf* statements to be obeyed. When executing the function *bigH* of 2.3, seven function calls are executed and each call causes a *printf* statement to be obeyed. For examples of this size we are unlikely to notice the difference in compile time or execute time between 2.2 and 2.3. If we were able to measure such times accurately then we would find that 2.2 compiled more slowly than 2.3, but executed more quickly. Our guideline, while approximate, will be that where symbols are replaced by small amounts of text then the symbol will be defined in a *define* statement, otherwise the symbol will be defined as a function. In contrast, if we knew that a function with a small body was called in a part of the program that was heavily used, then we would consider replacing the function definition by a *define* statement for the symbol name. This would save the overhead of the function call at execution time.

The ANSI standard allows functions defined in the standard libraries to have *#define* macro equivalents, provided that the libraries also contain the appropriate functions. This arrangement gives the programmer flexibility in deciding whether to use functions or macros even in the case of standard library constructs. By undefining the name of a macro using *#undef* directive, the programmer makes sure that a "real" function is used. Without the un-define, the program may be using a function or a macro depending on a particular C implementation.

## USING ARGUMENTS AND PARAMETERS

Functions are much more useful if we are able to pass information to them. Information can be passed implicitly, by using within the function symbol names that are defined elsewhere, or explicitly, by using parameters. The word "parameters" refers to the symbol names that are specified in the function definition; "arguments" are the actual values supplied when the function is called. The examples of *printf* used to date have been limited in that they simply print a given string. However, *printf* is a much more versatile function than these early examples suggest. In particular it can be made to print the value of data items that are passed as arguments, thus:

```
printf ("%c    %c\n" , '*','*');
```

The first argument must always be the string (in double quotes) that contains characters to be printed, formatting information, and conversion characters. The percent sign % precedes conversion characters in the string. More details of the conversion characters will be given in chapter 3. For the moment it will be enough to know that the letter c after % indicates a character conversion. For each conversion character in the control string a suitable argument must be provided within *printf* following the control string. Each parameter following the control string must have a corresponding conversion character within the control string. The *printf* statement given above has exactly the same effect as the *printf* statement given in function *endstars* of 2.3. We are now in a position to add a useful parameter to those functions that we have defined.

## DEFINING PARAMETERS

Consider the following version of *endstars*:

```
endstars (anychar)
char   anychar;
{
     printf ("%c    %c\n", anychar, anychar);
}
```

Here the function, *endstars*, is defined as having a parameter. The type of the parameters, if there is one  or more, can be defined before the brace which marks the start of the function body, or inside the parentheses containing the list of parameters. The latter style has been introduced by the C standard and will be described in detail in the section describing function prototypes in this chapter.

The parameters may then be used in a manner consistent with their definition anywhere within the function body. The function *endstars* simply uses *anychar* as an argument to *printf*. Hence whatever character is passed to *endstars* through the argument list in a function call is printed in the manner that should now be familiar.

*Example 2.4*

```
#include "adm5.h"
#define  GAP printf("\n\n\n\n")

main ()
{
    HOME; CLEAR; GAP; /* clear screen */
    bigH ('H');  GAP; /* use H to construct letter H */
    bigI ('I');  GAP; /* use I to construct letter I */
}

bigH (ch)
char ch;
{
    endstars (ch); endstars (ch); endstars (ch);
    allstars (ch);
    endstars (ch); endstars (ch); endstars (ch);
}
bigI (ch)
char ch;
{
    allstars (ch);
    midstar (ch); midstar (ch);
    midstar (ch); midstar (ch); midstar (ch);
    allstars (ch);
}

/* allstars(), endstars(), midstar()   */
/* are now defined as functions,        */
/* each has one parameter of type char */

allstars (ch)
char ch;
{ printf ("%c%c%c%c%c\n", ch, ch, ch, ch, ch); }

endstars (ch)
char ch;
{ printf ("%c   %c\n", ch, ch); }

midstar (ch)
char ch;
{ printf ("  %c  \n", ch); }

[ style 51.9 ]
```

If all the functions of the example 2.3 are parameterised in this fashion, and the corresponding calls are suitably amended, then we obtain a program such as 2.4. This program is more versatile than the others in the series in that by changing the character that is the actual argument to *bigH*, or to *bigI*, we can change the output produced. Using parameters in this way will usually help to make quite clear what must be passed from the caller to the function. If communication between a caller and a function is done implicitly by use of symbols to which both have access, the communication is not so obvious to the reader. For this reason early examples within the book will use the parameter list. Later examples will not be restricted in this way.

A further example of a function with parameters is one that enables us to move the cursor on the VDU screen to any position. For the ADM5 this function definition might appear as

```
/* to move the cursor to 'row', 'pos' */
cursor (row, pos)
int row, pos ;
{
    const int us = 31;      /* initialise for ADM5 */
    printf ("\033=%c%c", us+row, us+pos);
}
```

The call

```
cursor (1, 1);
```

would move the cursor to the 'home' position, while the call

```
cursor (12, 40);
```

would move the cursor to the middle of the screen. However, all of our other screen control directives are gathered together in an *include* file. The logical place for *cursor* is within that file too. But *cursor* needs parameters and so far none of the symbols in a *define* directive has used parameters. Recall that replacement of defined symbols is undertaken by a macroprocessor and, fortunately, this offers us parameter replacement. Hence the addition to our file of the following definition

```
#define CURSOR(r, p) printf("\033=%c%c", 31+r, 31+p)
```

will perform exactly the same role as the function of the same name.


## USING *return*

As well as passing information to a function, we must be able to pass information back to the caller from the function. This may be done in one of three ways: by using a *return* statement to pass a value via the function name, by passing one or more values back through the parameter list, or by changing the values of symbols to which both the function and the caller have access. For the reason given earlier this last form of communication will not yet be used.

The function *surface* in example 2.5 computes the surface area of a rectangular box having dimensions that can be expressed as integers. The value computed is communicated to the caller by the *return* statement and can be thought of as being associated with the function name. The function call can, in consequence, be used in expressions. In particular the call may appear in a *printf* statement, as indicated in example 2.5.

*Example 2.5*

```
main ()
{
    int length, width, depth;

    length = 10 ; width = 16 ; depth = 4;
    printf ("surface area = ");
    printf ("%d\n", surface (length, width, depth));

    return (0);
}

/***********************************/
/* to compute the surface area     */
/*    of a rectangular box         */
/***********************************/

surface (len, wid, dep)
int len, wid, dep;
{
    return (2*(len*wid + wid*dep + dep*len));
}
```

[ style 53.3 ]

Even such an apparently simple example raises several new points. The conversion character following the percent sign is d to indicate a decimal integer. In other respects the *printf* statement is little different from those already seen. The function definition has three parameters of integer type (*int*). The function call has three arguments of integer type. The parameters and arguments correspond in order, number and type  The function body consists simply of a *return* statement which computes the surface area.  So that no confusion arises in these early examples, the parameters have been given names that are different from the names of the arguments. The names leave no doubt as to which parameter corresponds to which argument.

The *return* statement passes a single value from the function to the caller. The type of this value is determined by the form of the expression in the *return* statement and the type of the operands.  If the returned value is of type integer or character (*char*) then the function definition is as given in example 2.5. However if the parameters to the function were of type *float* then the program should appear as in example 2.6.

The *main* function of any program is called by the underlying operating system and is always defined as returning a value of type *int*. Some operating systems interpret the value returned by the program at the completion of the *main* function and may act upon it. By convention, the return value of 0 signifies a normal successful program termination. Hence, we include the statement *return (0);* at the end of *main*.

*Example 2.6*

```
main ()
{
    float length, width, depth;

    float surface();  /* this is needed */

    length = 20.0; width = 26.0; depth = 4.0;
    printf ("surface area = ");
    printf ("%f\n", surface (length,width,depth));

    return (0);
}

/* this version of surface returns */
/* a result of type float         */

float
surface (len, wid, dep)
float len, wid, dep;
{ return (2*(len*wid + wid*dep + dep*len)); }

[ style 51.8 ]
```

The type of the arguments and the parameters has been changed to *float*. The function must now return a value that is also of type *float*. The type of result returned by the function is signalled by preceding the function name in the function definition by the type of value to be returned. A function is assumed by default to have the type *int*. If it is our intention to use a function that violates this assumption then we must signal this intention. This is done by including, in the functions or files that call this function, a declaration of the function. It is for this reason that an additional line appears

```
    float surface();
```

In addition to function declarations, ANSI C allows function prototypes which explicitly specify the number and type of parameters as explained in the next section.

## FUNCTION PROTOTYPES

Any function not explicitly declared in a program is assumed to return a value of type *int*. Obviously even the functions returning integer values can be declared to make this fact explicit. Before ANSI C, function declarations did not, however, specify the types and order of parameters and as a consequence it is very common in C programs to confuse the order or type of arguments in function calls and introduce errors which are often quite disastrous and difficult to diagnose. ANSI C solves this problem by introducing function prototyping which is possibly the single most important feature of the C standard.

Function prototypes may be viewed as business cards which introduce the function and its intended use. The function itself may be defined in another file as seen in several examples in the previous chapter, but the function prototype given in the program segment in which calls to the function are made ensures that the source program translator is aware of the order and type of function arguments and can diagnose any misuse of them. Function prototypes are given by specifying the type of the returned value, the function name and a list of types of formal parameters the function takes.

```
float volume (float, float, float);
static float surface (float radius);
void provide_answer (void);
int my_print (int number, float value, ...);
```

The above examples illustrate several important characteristics of function prototypes. Function *volume* is defined as returning a floating point value and taking three floating point parameters. An attempt to call the function with integer arguments will cause the corresponding arguments to be automatically converted to floating point values before the call is made. Function *surface* is defined as returning a floating point value and by the virtue of being *static*, will not be visible to functions in files other than the one containing its definition. The parameter name *radius* following the type definition is not necessary but is allowed for documentation purposes and in this case is useful in deciding that the function returns a value for a surface of a spherical object. Function *provide_answer* is of type *void* to indicate that the function does not return any value. The function is thus equivalent to procedures in some other programming languages. This function does not take any arguments either, as indicated by *void* parameter type. Please note that the prototype for *provide_answer* is not equivalent to a declaration such as

```
void provide_answer();
```

The former one explicitly specifies that the function does not take any arguments, whereas the latter is just a function declaration without any parameters specified and the function thus declared may or may not take arguments.

Finally, function *my_print* is specified to return an integer value and to take at least two arguments of type *int* and *float* respectively, possibly followed by other arguments. Any type checking performed by the compiler will be limited to the first two arguments of the function, in effect providing functions with variable number of arguments. The ellipsis indicating an unspecified number of arguments must always be the last parameter in the function definition. Ellipses in function prototypes combine the safety of specifying the parameter types with the flexibility afforded by providing only function definitions.

To take a full advantage of function prototypes and type checking performed by an ANSI C compiler, it is recommended that all functions of a program be prototyped, possibly in a separate header file or files and included as necessary in all the modules calling the corresponding functions. The task of providing such prototypes is made easier by a new format of function parameter definitions allowed by standard C.

*Example 2.7*

```
static float surface (float r); /* prototype of surface */

int
main ()
{
    float r;

    /* call to surface - %g indicates
       a floating point conversion */

   ·printf ("Surface for radius %g is %g\n", r, surface (r));

    return (0);
}

/*****************************
 *  Function to calculate    *
 *  surface area of a sphere *
 *****************************/
static float
surface (float r) /* definition of surface - no ";" */
{
    const float pi = 3.1415927;

    return (4*pi*r*r);          /* it's a sphere */
}

[ style 32.9 ]
```

In the above example, the parameter definition for *surface* is given inside the parentheses in both the function prototype and the function definition. The difference between formats of function prototypes and definitions lies only in the absence of the delimiting semicolon in the function definition and the opening brace indicating the beginning of the body of the definition. The old style of defining the types of formal parameters outside of the parentheses and before the opening brace is still allowed but discouraged. As with other new features introduced by the C standard, one may decide not to use them given that there are still many compilers which are not strictly conformant. In chapter 10 we will present some techniques which may be used to write strictly portable programs and yet allow the programs to be successfully compiled by the older, non standard compilers.

# RETURNING VALUES VIA THE PARAMETER LIST

As well as receiving data values through the parameter list it is also reasonable to expect that we can communicate data values back to the caller through one or more parameters. In order to understand the mechanism by which this is achieved, let us observe that in C all parameters are value parameters. That is, the values of the actual parameters are copied into temporary storage in the function work space upon entering the function. Thereafter, the function only makes reference to these local values. If assignment is made within the function body to one of the parameters, it will be the local copy that is changed, not the original. At first sight this seems to inhibit communication from the function to the caller via the parameter list. For C the way out is to use the address of the relevant data item.

# ADDRESSES AND POINTERS

| Address | Contents |
|---------|----------|
| &i      | i        |
| ptr     | *ptr     |

In a high-level language it is not usually necessary to know or care about the address in memory of the data values that we wish to manipulate. As a consequence, in some languages we have to resort to subterfuge in order to access specific memory locations. Pascal is one such language. At the other extreme, if it is too easy to access and modify memory locations then a program exploiting this facility can become unreadable. Thus a BASIC program which makes too much use of 'peek' and 'poke' instructions is not easily intelligible. In C an easy and convenient way of obtaining the address of a data item is provided. Correspondingly, given the address of a data item, we can easily obtain its value. As might be expected, in C the mechanism is short and simple. We obtain the address of an item by prefixing it with ampersand: thus &x is the address of x. In order that we can manipulate addresses we need to be able to define items that have pointers or addresses as their values. This is done as follows

```
int i ;    /* i represents a value of type integer */
int *ptr;  /* ptr holds the address of a data item */
           /* of type integer.

           /* an alternative declaration with the  */
           /* same effect follows                  */
int i, *ptr;
```

This notation can now be used to enable a function to communicate with its caller. For if the caller passes to the function the address of a data item, it is the address that is stored in the local storage area of the function. The function

cannot change the address of the item, but it can change the contents of the
address which is, after all, what we wish to happen. Example 2.5 may now be
rewritten as example 2.8.

*Example 2.8*

```
void
surface (int len, int wid, int dep, int *addr);

main ()
{
    int length, width, depth, area;

    length = 10; width = 16; depth = 4;
    surface (length, width, depth, &area);
    printf ("surface area = %d\n", area);

    return (0);
}

/* the fourth parameter is an address */
/* we refer to its contents as *addr   */

void
surface (int len, int wid, int dep, int *addr)
{ *addr = 2 * (len*wid + wid*dep + dep*len); return; }

[ style 39.7 ]
```

The differences between this example and the two previous examples need to
be highlighted. In the function *surface* the formal parameter *addr* is used to
communicate the computed surface area back to the caller. In order that this
may happen the contents of *addr*, *\*addr*, is typed as an integer which means
that *addr* is an address. The caller must therefore provide the address of an
integer type variable as the fourth argument. In the example it is the address of
*area*, *&area*, that is provided. Since the function is defined as *void* no value is
associated with the function name. Accordingly the function call is a statement
in the main segment of the example.

When a function has only one value to communicate to the caller it will
usually be convenient to use a *return* statement to pass the value via the
function name. If more than one value is to be communicated to the caller,
then we can use both the return mechanism and the parameter list, or we can
use the parameter list alone. Functions exhibiting these features will be used
later in the book when further language constructs have been introduced.

## SUMMARY

In this chapter, we have introduced two methods of abbreviating the number of statements that a programmer must write to produce a program: *defines* and functions. Choosing between the two is largely a matter of personal taste, subject to the guidelines that we have laid down.

Functions represent a major aid both to the modular development of a program and to its subsequent readability. The length of a function is again a matter of taste; ideally, a function should perform a single task, and should rarely, if ever, exceed a printed page in size.

We have discussed the various methods by which the functions of a program can communicate with each other. Suitable use of parameters not only generalises the use of a function, but also assists in an understanding of its purpose and the extent to which different parts of a program fit together.

# 3 Output and Input

## OUTPUT

Our use of the output function *printf* has so far been straightforward. We have seen that, as well as printing text strings, it can easily be made to convert the internal form of our data items into a suitable form for printing. The general form of the *printf* function call can be expressed as

```
printf (control_string [, argument_list])
```

(The square brackets enclose an item that is optional.) The control string may contain characters to be printed, special control characters preceded by backslash, and conversion specifiers.

## printf CONVERSION SPECIFIERS

For each conversion specifier there must be a corresponding argument in the argument list. The minimal form of a conversion specifier is a percent sign followed by one of a limited set of characters. Examples of conversion specifiers are given in table 3.1.

The general form of the conversion specifier can be written

```
%[ff][fw][.pp][mm]C
```

where    ff    is a set of optional flags which modify the meaning of the conversion specification as follows:

−     the result of the conversion will be left justified within the field. If "−" is not present, the result will be right justified.

+     the result of a signed conversion will always begin with a "+" or "-" sign. If "+" is not present, the result will be preceded by a sign only if a negative value is converted.

# the result is converted to an alternate form. For o conversion, nonzero result will have a 0 prefixed to it. For x and X conversions 0x or 0X will be prefixed to the result respectively.

0   the result of a numeric conversion will be prefixed with zeros to the specified field width.

fw  is a digit string giving the minimum field width - the total number of print positions occupied. Excess places in the field are by default filled with blanks, unless 0 flag is specified for numeric conversions. A data value that is too large for the field specified is printed in its entirety. An asterisk used instead of the digit string signifies that the field width is given by an integer (constant or variable) in the appropriate position in the argument list.

separates fw from pp.

pp  is a digit string which for a data item of type *float* or *double* specifies the number of digits to be printed after the decimal point. For a string it specifies the maximum number of characters from the string to be printed. For integer conversions, it specifies the minimum number of digits to be printed. As in the case of fw above, an asterisk can be used instead of the digit string.

mm  is one of h, l or L modifiers. h modifier specifies that the following integer conversion takes a *short* argument. l specifies that the following integer conversion takes a *long* argument. L specifies that the following floating point conversion takes a *long double* argument.

C   is the conversion character as specified in Table 3.1.

Table 3.1

| Conversion characters | Argument type | Comment |
|:---:|:---:|:---|
| c | char | Single character |
| d or i | int | Signed (if negative) decimal |
| u | int | Unsigned decimal |
| o | int | Unsigned octal, leading zeros suppressed |
| x or X | int | Unsigned hexadecimal. *abcdef* are used for *x* conversion, *ABCDEF* for *X* |
| f | float or double | Decimal notation |
| e or E | float or double | Scientific notation. Exponent is introduced by *e* or *E* respectively. |
| g or G | float or double | Shortest of %e, %f |
| s | string | |
| p | void* | Memory address is printed |
| n | int* | Number of characters written so far will be stored in the variable specified in the argument list. |
| % | *none* | % is written; that is, %% causes a single % to be printed. |

Any invalid conversion character is printed!

The examples in the text so far have used few of the option facilities listed above. If our programs are to produce acceptable output then we must be able to take full advantage of the facilities offered by *printf*. Much the best way to obtain the necessary familiarity is to use, and experiment with, different conversion specifiers. To help in this a list of examples is given in table 3.2.

## BACKSLASH

Within the control string we have used the backslash character preceding n to force the printing of a newline. There are other characters which have special significance when preceded by the backslash. The full list is given in table 3.3.

Table 3.2

| Value | Control String | : | Output | : |
|-------|----------------|---|--------|---|
| 360 | %10d | : | 360: | |
| -1 | %10ld | : | -1: | |
| 360 | %-10d | :360 | | : |
| -1 | %10hu | : | 65535: | |
| -1 | %10lu | :4294967295: | | |
| 360 | %10o | : | 550: | |
| -1 | %10lo | :37777777777: | | |
| 360 | %010o | :0000000550: | | |
| 360 | %-10x | :168 | | : |
| 360 | %-#10x | :0x168 | | : |
| 360 | %-#10X | :0X168 | | : |
| -1 | %-10lx | :ffffffff | | : |
| -1 | %-10lX | :FFFFFFFF | | : |
| 360 | %-010x | :1680000000: | | |
| 3.14159265 | %10f | : | 3.141593: | |
| 3.14159265 | %10.3f | : | 3.142: | |
| 3.14159265 | %-10.3f | :3.142 | | : |
| 3.14159265 | %10.0f | : | 3: | |
| 3.14159265 | %10g | : | 3.14159: | |
| 3.14159265 | %10e | :3.141593e+00: | | |
| 3.14159265 | %10.2e | : | 3.14e+00: | |
| programmer | %10s | :programmer: | | |
| programmers | %10s | :programmers: | | |
| programmer | %10.7s | : | program: | |
| programmer | %-10.7s | :program | | : |
| programmer | %10.4s | : | prog: | |
| programmer | %10.0s | :programmer: | | |
| programmer | %.3s | :pro: | | |

Table 3.3

| | |
|---|---|
| \a | alert (bell) |
| \b | backspace |
| \f | form feed |
| \n | newline (line feed) |
| \r | carriage return |
| \t | tab |
| \v | vertical tab |
| \ddd | ascii character code in octal |
| \xddd | ascii character code in hexadecimal |
| \' | ' |
| \" | " |
| \? | ? |
| \\ | \ |

The features of the *printf* statement that have been itemised are sufficient to provide the user with good control over the output generated. Remembering also that through the control string itself we can separate one field from another, we appear to have everything we need. It is now easy to modify example 2.1 so that it will print its large letters in the middle of the screen instead of on the lefthand side. All that is necessary is to ensure that, say, thirty-six leading spaces are printed before every string that is printed. This could be done by changing the first %c of each control string to %37c. If this proved unsatisfactory for some reason we would need to change each occurrence of 37 to something new. It will be much more convenient to use a *define* directive of the form

```
#define indent printf("%36c", ' ')
```

which will give us 36 leading spaces, and place the statement

```
indent;
```

before each of the relevant *printf* calls. A change in the number of leading spaces is now conveniently obtained by changing the value of one numeric constant.

## INPUT

So far our primary concern has been the organisation of our output. We must also be able to supply our program with data when it is executing. Corresponding to the output function *printf* is the input function *scanf* which has a similar philosophy. If we continue with the assumption that input and output are done through a VDU then a call to *scanf* of the form

```
scanf ("%d %d %d", &length, &width, &depth);
```

could have been used in example 2.5 to give values to the identifiers. The user would then need to type three integers as input when the program started to execute. Notice that because *scanf* must be able to communicate the input values to the caller, the caller must provide the address of the symbols to which the values are to be assigned. The general form of *scanf* is

```
scanf (control_string [, argument_list])
```

Within the control string blanks, tabs or newlines (collectively known as 'white space') cause the input to be read up to the first non-white-space characer. If any characters, apart from those needed in the conversion specifiers, appear in the control string, it is assumed that they are to match the next non-white-space character of the input stream. In particular, if any such characters appear as the first items in the control string then *scanf*, whenever it is called, will expect to find just these characters as the next to be read from the input stream. If the characters are not found, *scanf* fails, and the subsequent characters are not read.

## scanf CONVERSION SPECIFIERS

For *scanf* the conversion specifier has the following general form

```
%[*][dd][mm]C
```

where C is the conversion character, * is an optional assignment suppression character, dd represents a digit string giving the maximum field width, and mm is a modifier as in the case of printf. The characters admissible as conversion characters are given in table 3.4.

Table 3.4

| Conversion characters | Argument type |
| --- | --- |
| c | Pointer to char |
| d or i | Pointer to int |
| o | Pointer to int |
| x | Pointer to int |
| f | Pointer to float or double |
| e | Pointer to float or double |
| g | Pointer to float or double |
| s | Pointer to array of char |
| [.....] | Pointer to array of char |
| p | Pointer to void |
| n | Pointer to int |

Consider the following simple example

```
scanf ("%d", &fw);        /* read an integer 'fw'  */
printf ("%*c\n", fw, '+'); /* print a plus sign in  */
                          /* a field width of 'fw' */
```

An input field is normally delimited by white space characters, and hence for our first example of the use of *scanf* the three integers required for input could have been typed on a line separated by one or more spaces, or they could have been typed one per line. Either form, or a mixture of the two, would be acceptable. Be warned that this means that *scanf* will read across input lines to find the next item of data. If the conversion specifier includes the assignment suppression character, no assignment is made; in other words the corresponding input field is matched and skipped. Should the length of the input field exceed the fieldwidth specified, then the data item is assumed to consist of the first 'fieldwidth' characters. Example 3.1 will perhaps help to clarify some of these points.

*Example 3.1*

```
char  ch;
char  string[20];
int   i, j, extension;
long number;
float x;

    /* assume the input string PHONE65201X4133           */

scanf ("PHONE %ld %c %d", &number, &ch, &extension);
    /* yields number = 65201, ch = 'X', extension = 4133  */

scanf ("PHON %c %f %*c %d", &ch, &x, &ch, &extension);
    /* yields ch = 'E', x = 65201.0, extension = 4133     */

scanf ("PHONE %2d %3d %c %2f", &i, &j, &ch, &x);
    /* yields i = 65, j = 201, ch = 'X', x = 41.0         */

scanf ("%[^X] %c %d", string, &ch, &extension);
    /* yields string = "PHONE65201", ch = 'X',
                                  extension = 4133      */

scanf ("PHONE %[0123456789] %c %d", string, &ch, &extension);
    /* yields string = "65201", ch = 'X',
                                  extension = 4133      */
```

Note that in the third example *scanf* has not read the last two characters (33) of the input stream. The next call to *scanf* would scan from the first of these characters. If the input stream contains nothing to match the current item of the control string, *scanf* terminates. Termination also occurs when all elements of the control string have been satisfied.

A variation on the string conversion specification is introduced in the last two examples, where the string is not delimited by white space characters. The specifier %[...] indicates a string containing any of the characters within the square brackets (and delimited by any that is not), while the specifier %[^...] indicates a string delimited by the character set within brackets.

*scanf* returns to the caller the number of data items that were matched and assigned. A value of zero is returned when the next character of the input stream does not match the first item in the control string, and the value EOF (defined in stdio.h) is returned when end of file is encountered. Thus if the call to *scanf* in the third example appeared instead as

```
items = scanf ("PHONE %2d %3d %c %2f", &i, &j, &ch, &x);
```

then *items* would be assigned the value 4.

The input stream searched by *scanf* is the standard input stream *stdin*. The output produced by *printf* is directed to the standard output *stdout*. It will frequently be necessary to scan other data sources and to direct output to other destinations. This can easily be achieved by using variants of *scanf* and *printf*. One of these variants allows us to deal with strings.

## STRINGS

In C a string constant is a sequence of characters enclosed in double quotes. Like other data items strings may be read in, stored, manipulated and printed. Strings are stored in arrays of characters (this topic is covered in detail in chapter 7) and are referenced by the address of the first character, a pointer to array of char. The general form of the version of *scanf* that processes strings is

```
sscanf (data_string, control_string [, argument_list])
```

*sscanf* scans the string *data_string* attempting to match the data items specified in the control string. Successful matches are, when appropriate, assigned to the arguments in the argument list. Correspondingly

```
sprintf (data_string, control_string [, argument_list])
```

writes the arguments specified in the argument list into the data string in the manner determined by the control string. Since we can refer to strings only by means of a pointer to an array of char, it is obvious that the first argument to *sprintf* is the address of the data item that is to be changed.

## I/O FUNCTION LIBRARY

The C language standard requires that there will exist a library of functions to perform various input/output tasks. All such functions are defined in the standard, in effect introducing into the language a set of reserved names. Both *printf* and *scanf* are defined in this library.

The functions *getchar* and *putchar* should be part of any non-standard C library and, as their names imply, they communicate single characters from and to the VDU which we are assuming to be our input/output device. For example

```
ch = getchar (); /* get next character */
putchar (ch);    /* print it */
```

or, equivalently

```
putchar (ch = getchar ());
```

since, in C, an assignment is an expression that yields the value assigned as its result.

The input/output functions that will usually form part of any non-standard runtime library are listed in table 3.5. Chapter 12 lists all the functions which must be defined in any strictly conformant C implementation. Any function not defined in a particular version of a C library and thought to be important or useful can be added to such a library by the user. If any such additions are made, it is obviously desirable that the functions providing functionality defined in the standard be constructed in a strictly conformant way. This would include the names of functions and libraries, the names of header files, purpose of the functions and order and type of parameters taken. Any functions not defined in the standard but useful or necessary for a particular implementation should draw on the standard and be implemented in a way consistent with it. Examples of such libraries include machine dependant functions such as port operations or graphics for the PC family, or site specific functions such as special mathematical or statistical functions. There is no suggestion that even in the case of non-conformant implementations, the list in table 3.5 gives all, and only, those functions that should appear in the library.

When viewed collectively the functions listed in table 3.5 leave one wondering why

(1) the names *putc, getc* are not *fputc, fgetc* to indicate that they communicate with files, and

(2) the *file_pointer* argument of *putc, fputs, fgets* does not appear as the first argument as it does in *fprintf, fscanf*.

The following definitions might help the user whose sense of order is offended.

```
#define fputc(f, a)            putc(a, f)
#define fgetc(f)               getc(f)
#define fputstring(f, a)       fputs(a, f)
#define fgetstring(f, a1, a2)  fgets(a1, a2, f)
```

## FILE I/O

We have explicitly assumed so far that our input or output takes place from or to the user's terminal. While this will suffice for much initial work, we will wish, ultimately, to be able to read from and write to files. There are three files that are always available to any program. These are *stdin*, *stdout* and *stderr*, the files for standard input, standard output and standard error messages. In practice these three files are always linked to the user's terminal. These files are opened at program entry and closed at program exit.

Table 3.5

```
printf (control_string [, argument_list])
scanf (control_string [, argument_list])

putchar (argument)
getchar ()

sprintf (data_string, control_string [, argument_list])
sscanf (data_string, control_string [, argument_list])

fprintf (file_pointer, control_string [, argument_list])
fscanf (file_pointer, control_string [, argument_list])

putc (argument, file_pointer)
getc (file_pointer)

fputs (argument, file_pointer)
fgets (argument1, argument2, file_pointer)
```

Users wishing to use other files must perform the opening and closing themselves. Functions are provided to simplify this work. Opening a file involves passing a file name together with other information to the function *fopen* which returns a pointer to a file. Input/output functions using this pointer may write to a file or read from a file. The functions *fprintf* and *fscanf* are, apart from the fact that they communicate with a file, identical in action to their counterparts *printf* and *scanf*. The general form of their calls is given in table 3.5.

## CLOSING A FILE

As part of the housekeeping associated with our program, a file should be closed when it is no longer needed. This is done by a call to the function *fclose* which has a general form

```
fclose (file_pointer)
```

When a program terminates normally, all open files are closed automatically.

## OPENING A FILE

The operating system under which a C program executes may impose a limit on the number of files that the program may have open at one time. You should establish whether such a limit exists for your system and ascertain its value. If this limit is inadvertently exceeded, a warning should be given when opening the file that causes the limit to be passed. Since other problems also could arise in opening a file, such as 'file does not exist', 'file is write protected', and so on, it is worth having a closer look at the details of opening a file.

A file pointer points to a data item that we have not so far encountered, an object of type FILE. This is not a simple data item such as one with type *char* or *int* that we have used previously, but is more complex. We need not know what data items the type FILE embraces. A file of standard definitions of items essential to the input/output functions is kept in the include file 'stdio.h'. By including this file in our program, we define such symbols as FILE, EOF and NULL. For local use within the program we need a file pointer, which we will call *fptr*, and we need to use *fopen* to open the required file. The general form of a call to *fopen* is

```
fopen (file_name, file_mode)
```

This function returns a file pointer to the file that has been opened. Since the function is therefore not returning a value of the default type (*int* or *char*), it must be declared within the function, or file, that is to use it. This is done by including *stdio.h* header file which in standard C provides prototypes for all input/output functions. The prototype for *fopen* is of the form

```
FILE *fopen (const char *filename, const char *mode);
```

where *const* means that the parameters will in no way be modified by the call to the function. Our modified program of example 2.1 looks now like this:

*Example 3.2*

```
#include "adm5.h"
#include <stdio.h>

#define GAP fprintf(fptr, "\n\n\n\n")

#define allstars fprintf(fptr, "*****\n")
#define endstars fprintf(fptr, "*   *\n")
#define midstar fprintf(fptr, "  *  \n")

FILE *fptr;

main ( )
{
    fptr = fopen ("results.text", "w");
    if (fptr == NULL) {
        printf (" error in opening file\n");
    } else {
        HOME; CLEAR;  GAP;
        bigH ();     GAP;
        bigI ();     GAP;
        fclose (fptr);
    }

    return (0);
}
```

```
bigH ()
{
    endstars; endstars; endstars;
    allstars;
    endstars; endstars; endstars;
}
bigI ()
{
    allstars;
    midstar; midstar; midstar; midstar; midstar;
    allstars;
}

[ style 67.9 ]
```

The *filename* argument to *fopen* must be a string giving the name of the file to be opened. The *mode* argument must also be a string which specifies the type of access required. Some possible file modes are

r       read access
w       write access
a       append access

An attempt to open a file that does not exist for writing or appending will result in the file being created. If a non-existent file is opened for reading, then *fopen* will return the value NULL. Other errors will also result in the NULL value being returned by *fopen*. As a result, if the file is opened by a statement such as:

```
fptr = fopen ("results.text", "w");
```

we must immediately check that the file pointer *fptr* in not NULL. This is done using a conditional statement, and while this has not yet formally been introduced, it should be clear from the example that a NULL return from *fopen* will cause our program to print an error message; a non-NULL return will cause it to continue execution normally.

There are some specific comments worth making about example 3.2. HOME and CLEAR have not been modified and so send their character sequences to the VDU and not to the results file. The FILE declaration must not be within a function since *main, bigH* and *bigI* all need to refer to *fptr*. *printf* has been changed to *fprintf* in the *define* directives and *fptr* has been added as the first parameter. The standard input/output definitions in 'stdio.h' have been included.

## SUMMARY

Output and input provide the interface between the program and its environment. Standard C specifies a rich variety of input/output functions implemented as a library which must be defined in any conformant C implementation. The program interface provided by this library, that is to say the form of the function calls and the effects of each function, is standardised and well defined. However, the individual implementation of these functions is by necessity different in various computing environments.

Even though some older, non-conformant C implementations may not provide all these functions, the input/output facilities that we have discussed in this chapter are generally accepted as a *de facto* standard. However, your local implementation should be checked before assuming that you can use the functions we have specified: your implementation may have either more or less than ours.

Since the principal function of all programs is to communicate, whether it be with other programs, devices, or the human user, as much thought should be given to the design of this interface as to the problem solution. It is not sufficient that a program produces the correct results, if those results, by virtue of poor presentation, are difficult to interpret; nor is it sufficient that a program assumes the integrity of its input, for this is usually the one factor over which the programmer has no control.

# 4 Decisions

A programming language that only offered the possibility of moving from one instruction to the next instruction in sequence would be extremely limiting. To be useful, we must be provided with the facility to choose different courses of action under different circumstances. There are two distinct ways that this may be done in C. We can use either the conditional statement or the *switch* statement.

## CONDITIONAL STATEMENT

Two forms of the conditional statement are available in C:

```
if (expression) statement1
if (expression) statement1 else statement2
```

An example of the latter form appears in example 3.2 to test that a file has been opened satisfactorily.

If the conditional statement currently under discussion is included, the kind of statements used so far in the text include

- an assignment expression,
- a function call,
- a conditional statement,
- a return statement, and
- a compound statement.

(Recall that a compound statement is a group of statements enclosed by braces {}). Any of the statement types listed can be used as indicated by the general form of the conditional statement. Other forms of statement, defined later, can also be used. With the exception of the compound statement in the list above, all statements are terminated by a semi-colon. Anyone familiar with Pascal will find that the form of the conditional statement which uses *else* can, in certain circumstances, look strange. Different forms of the conditional statement are shown in example 4.1.

*Example 4.1*

```
if (n < 0)   printf ("n is negative\n");
if (n == 0) printf ("n is zero\n");
if (n > 0)   printf ("n is positive\n");

/*   since the three statements above are    */
/*   distinct conditional statements, all    */
/*   tests are always performed. In contrast */
/*   consider the following alternative;      */

if (n < 0) printf ("n is negative\n");
else if (n == 0) printf ("n is zero\n");
else printf ("n is positive\n");
```

What follows the comments in example 4.1 is a single conditional statement. The first *if* has a corresponding *else*, and what follows the *else* is a conditional statement. This way of expressing a condition may at first seem strange, but it will usually permit an elegant expression of our logic. In addition it is economical, in that, when one of the tests within the statement is satisfied and the corresponding action undertaken, execution of the conditional statement terminates.

The use of braces to signify a compound statement adds considerably to the expressive power of the conditional statement, in that the execution of groups of statements can be made dependent on a specific condition. This can perhaps be appreciated in example 3.2 where the main part of the program is executed only if the output file is opened satisfactorily.

Perhaps the part of the conditional statement that it is most important to understand is the condition itself. The general form of the statement showed this to be an expression enclosed by parentheses. Expressions will be considered in greater detail in chapter 6. For the present we can use the comparison of simple data items as an example of the form of expression required. An expression such as

```
n > 7
```

can be evaluated as soon as *n* is known. We expect the result *true* if *n* is greater than 7 and *false* otherwise. Convention dictates that we regard the value zero as *false* and non-zero as *true*. Thus, if the parenthesised expression following *if* yields a non-zero or *true* value the statement that immediately follows is executed, and the *else* part, if it exists, is ignored. However, if the parenthesised expression yields a zero or *false* value, the statement that follows *else* is executed. This property is exploited in the following function:

```
/* to determine whether 'ch' is */
/* the letter 'y', or 'Y'        */
```

```
int
affirmative (char ch)
{
    if (ch == 'y') return (1);
    else if (ch == 'Y') return (1);
    else return (0);
}
```

If the character passed to *affirmative* is an upper case or lower case 'y' the value 1 is returned, otherwise 0 is returned. Such a function can significantly help the readability of our program. For, after prompting the user for a single character reply *reply* to a question, we could then write:

```
if (affirmative (reply)) printf ("reply is yes\n");
```

Note that it is not necessary to compare the value returned by *affirmative* with zero or anything else. Indeed to do so would detract from the readability of the resulting statement. We could of course exploit the same principle by writing:

```
if (n) printf ("n is non-zero\n");
```

but we would argue that this is not good practice as *n* represents numeric values rather than the *true* or *false* values that affirmative represents. (For illustrative purposes, the body of *affirmative* is more verbose than it need be. This function would normally be written in C as:

```
int
affirmative (char ch)
{ return (ch == 'y' || ch == 'Y') }
```

where | | is the 'or' operator.)

## TRAPS FOR THE UNWARY

Consider the two statements

```
if (ch = 'Y') return (1);
if (ch == 'Y') return (1);
```

and ask whether you can clearly state what each does. They differ only in that the first has one less 'equals' sign than the second. There is, nonetheless, a significant difference in their actions. The second statement tests whether *ch* has the value 'Y', returns 1 if it does and continues with the next statement in sequence if it does not. In contrast the first statement assigns the value 'Y' to *ch* then, because an assignment is an expression that yields as its result the value assigned, the *return* statement is executed, since the parenthesised expression yields a non-zero value. This difference in action can be extremely important. Its advantage is that an assignment and a test of the assigned value are neatly combined. Its disadvantage is that if you intended comparison (==) rather than assignment (=) your program is logically incorrect but syntactically correct.

Those people moving to C from a language in which the single 'equals' sign is used for comparison are advised to check their conditional statements carefully.

## MULTIPLE CONDITIONS

Let us assume that we are given an integer, which is an examination mark, and that we are to translate this mark into a grade. An A grade is obtained for a mark in the range 80 to 99, B for a mark in the range 60 to 79, and so on. The null character is returned for a mark outside the range 0 to 99. There is, as usual, more than one way to achieve this end, but a look at several methods will help to contrast the use of different facilities in C.

*Example 4.2*

```
int
grade (int mark)
{
    char g;

    if (mark < 0 ) g = '\0';
    else if (mark < 20) g = 'E';
    else if (mark < 40) g = 'D';
    else if (mark < 60) g = 'C';
    else if (mark < 80) g = 'B';
    else if (mark < 100) g = 'A';
    else g = '\0';

    return (g);
}
[ style 47.9 ]
```

While the logic of the statement is simple and economical, it is lengthy. What is needed to deal with the problem of example 4.2 is a construct that offers a multiple choice of actions in contrast to the binary choice offered by the conditional statement. The *switch* statement is just such a construct.

## THE *switch* STATEMENT

The general form of the switch statement is

```
switch (expression) statement
```

The value yielded by the expression must be of integral type and will be used to select which of several statements to execute. The statement that follows the selecting expression will, if the switch is to serve any useful purpose, contain one or more statements preceded by

```
case constant_expression:
```

The constant expression can be thought of as labelling the statement that it prefixes. This statement is executed if the selecting expression yields a value that matches the constant expression. Within any *switch* statement the constant expression that labels a statement must be unique. A rewritten version of the mark grading example should make clear the form and logic of the *switch* statement.

*Example 4.3*

```
int
grade (int mark)
{
    char g;

    switch (mark / 20) {
        case 0: g = 'E'; break;
        case 1: g = 'D'; break;
        case 2: g = 'C'; break;
        case 3: g = 'B'; break;
        case 4: g = 'A'; break;
    }

    return (g);
}

[ style 49.5 ]
```

The unexpected feature of this example is, perhaps, the *break* statement. When it is encountered it causes exit from the *switch*. If in the example 4.3 the first *break* were omitted, then having assigned 'E' to g the next statement, which assigns 'D' to *g*, is executed. In other circumstances, as we shall see, we might wish to exploit this course of action. It is not appropriate to do so in this example - all the *break* statements, with the exception of the last, are essential.

Example 4.3 is logically similar to example 4.2. It is not identical in its action, as the null character is not returned if *mark* is outside the expected range. A statement prefixed by *default* is executed if the value produced by the switching expression does not match any of the constants following *case* within the switch statement. In example 4.3 when none of the *case* constants is matched exit is made from the *switch* statement. We can ensure that marks which are out of range are satisfactorily processed by including the statement:

```
default: g = NULL; break;
```

anywhere within the *switch* statement of example 4.3. Finally we note that no ordering of the *case* or *default* prefixes is necessary or implied. The example 4.4 should make these points clear.

*Example 4.4*

```
/* to determine whether a given character */
/* is a vowel. Zero is returned for non-  */
/* vowels. An integer in the range 1 to 5 */
/* is returned for a vowel.               */

int
vowel (char ch)
{
    switch (ch) {
        default: return (0);
        case 'u': case 'U': return (5);
        case 'a': case 'A': return (1);
        case 'e': case 'E': return (2);
        case 'i': case 'I': return (3);
        case 'o': case 'O': return (4);
    }
}

[ style 54.0 ]
```

This example exploits the fact that a *case* which is not followed by a *break* causes the following statement to be executed. In this way we can easily deal with both upper and lower case versions of the characters. The statement prefixed by *default* could as easily be the last statement of the switch as the first. Another feature exploited is the use of *return* rather than a *break* statement. *return* causes exit from the *switch* statement and from the function.

## SUMMARY

In this chapter we have discussed two of the constructs that give programming its flexibility - the two-way and multi-way branch. Strictly, from the point of view of the logic of a program, one of the constructs is unnecessary, since either can be expressed in terms of the other. Careful use of the appropriate construct can, however, considerably enhance the intelligibility of a program.

A two-way branch will almost always be implemented with a conditional statement; a multi-way branch can be implemented either by nested conditionals or by a *switch* statement. As a general rule, we can say that nested conditional statements should be used whenever we are testing a series of conditions in decreasing order of expected frequency; when all the conditions are equally likely to occur, a *switch* statement should be used.

# 5 Loops

The conditional statements of the previous chapter freed our programs from the straitjacket of the sequential execution of instructions without branching, but it is the ability to loop, or repeat the execution of one or more instructions, that brings power to programming. It brings economy too, for a modest number of programming language statements can be responsible for a significant amount of computing time.

C offers at least three ways in which we can construct loops. We can use a *while* statement, a *do* statement, or a *for* statement. Of these, the *while* statement is the most important, because it can be used to do anything that the other two loop constructs can do. The other two forms of loop construct are available because, in certain circumstances, they offer a more appropriate means of expressing our logic.

## THE *while* STATEMENT

The *while* statement has the general form:

```
while (expression) statement
```

The list of statements given at the start of chapter 4 must now be extended to include the *while* statement. Any one of this extended list of statements is admissible as the statement part of the general form of the *while* statement given above. The expression in parentheses has the same role as the parenthesised expression of the conditional statement - that is, it is evaluated and tested. If it produces a non-zero or *true* result, the statement that follows is executed. The expression is then tested again and, if *true*, the statement following is executed once more. This sequence is repeated until the evaluation of the expression yields a *false* result, and then the statement that follows the *while* statement is executed.

There is, of course, an implicit assumption that something occurs within the *while* loop which causes the value produced by the controlling expression to change at some time. The statement:

```
while (1) i = 0;
```

causes an infinite loop, setting *i* to zero interminably. Care must be taken to ensure that loops do terminate!

In example 5.1 we introduce two new operators, !=, and ++. The first tests for inequality; the second is the increment operator, which when used as in:

```
count++;
```

causes *count* to be incremented by one. Suppose our task is to count the number of characters on a line. Assuming that the input stream is positioned at the start of a line, the following statements perform the count:

```
count = 0;
ch = getchar ();

while (ch != '\n') {
    count++;
    ch = getchar ();
}
```

But these statements do not exploit some of the features that we have already seen. In particular, the test that controls the *while* statement could easily be modified to include the assignment to *ch*. The modified version uses this feature and is presented as a function.

*Example 5.1*

```
#include <stdio.h>

int
counter (void)
{
    char ch;
    int count = 0;

    while ((ch = getchar ()) != '\n')
        count++;
    return (count);
}

[ style 54.1 ]
```

Example 5.1 also capitalises upon the ability, in C, to initialise variables as part of their definition. A closer look at the function *counter* should prompt the realisation that *ch* is used only in the expression that controls the *while* loop. If this is so, then we should dispense with *ch* altogether and rewrite the function as in example 5.2.

*Example 5.2*

```
#include <stdio.h>

int
counter (void)
{
    int count = 0;

    while (getchar () != '\n')
        count++;
    return (count);
}
```

[ style 52.6 ]

In this, and other ways, C offers many aids to writing 'economical' (some would say terse) programs. The reader is encouraged to exploit these features but to bear in mind that simplicity and clarity of expression should not be sacrificed in order to produce 'smart', but not easily readable, programs.

## ESCAPING FROM LOOPS

The *break* statement, which was used to escape from the *switch* statement, will also force exit from a *while* statement. Following the execution of *break*, the statement that follows the *while* statement is executed. A *return* statement also may be used to escape from the *while* loop. However, as might be expected, this not only causes immediate exit from the *while* statement, but also forces exit from the function that contains the *while* statement.

The *while* statement can also be exploited when attempting to make the user interface of a program more robust. If a program directs a query to its user which requires a simple 'yes' or 'no' answer, for example:

```
Do you wish to continue (Y or N)?
```

then only the response indicated should be accepted. Consider example 5.3.

*Example 5.3*

```c
#include <stdio.h>

#define BELL '\7'

int
replyisyes (void)
{
    char ch;

    while (1) {
        ch = getchar ();
        switch (ch) {
            default: putchar (BELL); break;
            case 'y': case 'Y': return (1);
            case 'n': case 'N': return (0);
        }
    }
}
```

[ style 75.9 ]

Exit is only made from the function when 'Y' or 'N' of either upper or lower case is received. Receipt of any other character causes the VDU to 'beep' and, although exit is made from the *switch* statement, the *while* statement remains active.

This last example provides the opportunity to state again that a program's interface with its user is extremely important. If a question is directed to the user, ensure that the acceptable responses are made known, and write the program logic in such a way that only valid responses are accepted.

Further details of the input/output philosophy of the underlying operating system will need to be clarified before example 5.3 can be used conveniently. Usually, for example, a user is required to provide 'line at a time' input. That is, the underlying operating system buffers, or stores the characters typed until a 'newline' character is encountered. Only then the system sends the entire buffer, including the 'newline' character to the application. Example 5.3 would 'beep' at any character other than 'N', 'n', 'Y' or 'y', including any 'newline' characters that it encountered. It is usually possible to arrange 'character at a time' input.

The *while* loop is important because, as is evident from its structure, the controlling condition is tested before entering the loop. In contrast, the expression that controls the *do* loop is tested only at the end of the loop, and therefore the statement controlled by the loop is always executed at least once.

## THE *do* STATEMENT

The general form of the *do* loop is:

```
do statement while (expression)
```

Our list of statements must now be extended to include the *do* statement. Any one of the resulting list of statements is suitable as the statement used in the general form given above.

As an illustrative example, let us assume that we have access to a file containing one word per line. Our task is to sum, for each such word, the number of times that we find a vowel preceded by a consonant. The sum produced is a good approximation to the number of syllables in the word. We assume a file pointer *fptr*, and a function *consonant* which returns a non-zero (true) value if the character passed as a parameter is a consonant. The function *vowel* was given as example 4.4.

*Example 5.4*

```c
#include <stdio.h>

int
syllables (void)
{
    char ch;
    int changes = 0, previousvowel = 0;

    do {
        ch = getc (fptr);
        if (vowel (ch)) {
            if (!previousvowel)
                changes++;
            previousvowel = 1;
        } else if (consonant (ch))
            previousvowel = 0;
    } while (ch != '\n');

    return (changes);
}

[ style 69.8 ]
```

(As a syllable counter, the function of example 5.4 is limited in that there are special cases that it does not handle. Thus 'by' would be credited with having no syllables, and 'ale' with two. For most words, however, it is a good first approximation.)

## THE *for* STATEMENT

The *for* statement proves convenient to use when it is necessary to execute a loop a given number of times. While this could also be done by either of the other two loop constructs, we should select the statement that is most appropriate for the task. Counting through a loop requires three 'housekeeping' activities: initialising the counter, incrementing the counter, and testing whether the terminating value has been reached. It is helpful to both the reader and the writer of a program if these three housekeeping activities are collected together. This is economically achieved in the *for* statement which has the general form:

```
for (expression1; expression2; expression3) statement
```

where:

| | |
|---|---|
| expression1 | initialises the counter |
| expression2 | gives the continuing condition, and |
| expression3 | increments the counter. |

Thus to compute the sum of the first N natural numbers we could write:

```
sum = 0;
for (i = 1; i <= N; i++) sum = sum + i;
```

or, if it is more suitable to count down:

```
sum = 0;
for (i = N; i >= 1; i--) sum = sum + i;
```

In C, the statement controlled by the *for* statement in these examples can be more concisely written as:

```
sum += i;
```

## THE *continue* STATEMENT

We have seen that *break* will cause immediate exit from a *switch* or *while* statement. It will also cause immediate exit from a *do* statement or *for* statement. The loop statements (*while*, *do*, and *for*) can also use a *continue* statement. The *continue* statement is less drastic than the *break* statement because it only causes termination of the present iteration. If *continue* is encountered in the execution of *while* or *do* loops, it causes a branch to the loop control test to be made. In a *for* statement a *continue* causes execution of the 'increment' expression prior to testing whether another iteration of the loop is appropriate.

Imagine that a file contains a collection of marks, except that the very first number in the file gives the number of marks that follow. Using the function *grade* of example 4.2, we are to compute the number of pass grades in the mark list (example 5.5).

*Example 5.5*

```
#include <stdio.h>

/* fscanf may return EOF or zero; */
/* grade returns null if the      */
/*        mark is out of range;   */
/* only an E grade does not pass. */

int
passes (void)
{
    char g;
    int listsize, mark, m, psum=0;

    if (fscanf (fptr, "%d", &listsize) < 1) return (-1);

    for (m = 1; m <= listsize; m++) {
        if (fscanf (fptr, "%d", &mark) > 0) {
            if ((g = grade (mark)) == '\0') continue;
            if (g == 'E') continue;
            psum++;
        } else return (-1);
    }

    return (psum);
}

[ style 73.0 ]
```

## DYNAMIC CHANGE OF INCREMENT

The *for* statement in C is implemented in a manner that enables it to be used in some rather surprising ways. For example:

```
for ( ; ; ) k = 0;
```

represents an infinite loop. The assumption is made that, if the second expression, which is the controlling condition, is omitted, the value *true* is to be used. The most significant way that the *for* statement differs from the *for* statement as defined in, say Pascal, is that both the terminating condition and the increment expressions are re-evaluated for every iteration. This means that if the identifiers used in computing these values are changed within the *for* loop, then either the terminating condition, or the step size, or both, can be constantly changed from within the loop. Consider, for example:

```
for (p = 1; p <= 4096; p = 2*p) printf ("%4d\n", p);
```

which prints a small list of powers of two. It achieves this by multiplying the 'increment' by two each time through the loop.

The loop terminating condition need not involve the 'counter', although it usually will. The loop of example 5.2 could be rewritten, using a *for* statement, in the following form:

```
for (count = 0; getchar () != '\n'; count++);
```

Here the *for* statement has an empty statement part, because all the necessary work is done within the controlling expressions. Note that the terminating condition is independent of *count*. Changing the loop terminating condition from within the loop should be done carefully, if at all. There is a danger that it may be changed in such a way as to ensure that the loop never terminates at all.

A final example on *for* statements is used to show that they, or any of the other looping constructs, may be nested to create a loop within a loop. Example 5.6 computes 'perfect' numbers. If we exclude the number itself from a list of its factors, then a perfect number is the same as the sum of its factors, so that the first perfect number is 6, because the factors of 6 are 1, 2 and 3, and 1+2+3 = 6. It is only necessary to examine even numbers for perfection, because, although it remains to be formally proved, it is surmised that odd numbers cannot be perfect.

*Example 5.6*

```
#include <stdio.h>

#define LO    6       /* first perfect number */
#define HI    1000    /* limit of search */
int
main (void)
{
    int num, sum, factor;

    printf ("Perfect numbers\n");
    for (num = LO; num <= HI; num += 2) {
        sum = 1;
        for (factor = 2; factor < num; factor++)
            if (num % factor == 0)
                sum += factor;
        if (sum == num)
            printf ("%4d\n", num);
    }
}

[ style 67.4 ]
```

The modulus operator, %, is described in more detail in chapter 6. It gives, in this case, the remainder when *num* is divided by *factor*.

## THE *goto* STATEMENT

The loop structures introduced so far, if used properly, should mean that the user rarely, if ever, needs to use a *goto* statement. In particular, a *goto* need never be used to construct loops. However, in certain error situations, a *goto* may enable a cleaner program termination to take place. A statement may be labelled by prefixing it by an identifier followed by a colon. The *goto* statement may then use this label as its destination, thus:

```
goto abort;
    ....
    ....
abort: printf (" abnormal termination\n");
```

## SUMMARY

C's looping constructs correspond to those found in many other high-level languages. Usually, a determinate loop, where the number of iterations is known in advance, is most appropriately implemented by a *for* statement, while an indeterminate loop, where termination depends on some condition being satisfied, is better implemented as a *while* or a *do* statement. These are general rules, however, and, as has already been demonstrated, C's *for* statement is powerful enough to enable it to be effectively used to control an indeterminate loop under certain circumstances. This being so, it is wise to consider carefully which particular statement is likely to yield the most natural expression of the loop's intent.

# 6 Operators

In preceding chapters we have used identifiers with type *char*, *int*, and *float*. In addition, data types *void*, *short*, *long*, *double*, *signed*, *unsigned* and *long double* are provided in standard C. Most of these data types are also provided in most non-standard compilers. We suggest that you look at the implementation notes for C on your system to discover what is on offer.

## TYPE CONVERSION

The type names introduced above can conveniently be listed in order as follows:

```
void, char, short, int, long, float, double, long double
```

*signed* and *unsigned* can be used as types in themselves, in which case the object thus declared is considered to be either signed or unsigned *int* respectively. They can also be prefixed to any "integer" type, that is any of *char*, *short*, *int* and *long*, in which case the object is treated as either a signed or unsigned entity of a given type. Both *signed* and *unsigned* types are omitted from the above list. They can be treated simply as type modifiers to indicate whether the integers can be assigned positive and negative or positive only values. Type *int* is typically implemented to correspond in size to the word size of the underlying hardware and is equivalent to either *short* or *long* depending on the particular implementation. *void* type has been introduced in the ANSI standard and has meaning only in conjunction with function definitions and pointers. You will recall that in function definitions it specifies that the function does not return a value or does not take any parameters. You will also recall that pointers are addresses of other objects. A *void* pointer specifies that an address of an unknown object type is represented. As a result, a *void* pointer can contain an address of an object of any valid type. Apart from the *long/float* boundary and the *void* pointer, this list is in order of increasing storage size. By storage size we mean the amount of storage needed for a data item of the given type. With this list in mind the implicit type conversion rules given below can readily be understood.

For an expression involving one of the binary operators (one with two operands), such as:

```
a + b
```

the type of the result is determined by the type of the operands according to the following rules:

- if either operand is of type *long double*, the other operand is converted to *long double*;

- otherwise, if either operand is of type *double*, the other operand is converted to *double*;

- otherwise, if either operand is of type *float*, the other operand is converted to *float*;

- otherwise, integral promotions are performed as follows:
  *signed* and *unsigned* objects are initially converted to *int*, unless the conversion changes the value, in which case the object is converted to *unsigned int* (this is known as a value preserving conversion and has been adopted by the ANSI standard - non-conformant compilers may not perform this conversion); *char* and *short* are converted to *int*, provided that *int* can represent all values of the original type; otherwise the values are converted to *unsigned int*.

Following the integral promotions, all operands are in the 'int' family and the following rules are now applied:

- if either operand is of type *unsigned long int*, the other operand is converted to *unsigned long int*;

- otherwise, if either operand is of type *long int*, the other operand is converted to *long int*;

- otherwise, if either operand is of type *unsigned int*, the other operand is converted to *unsigned int*;

- otherwise, both operands are of type *int*.

After applying the above rules, both operands are of the same type and the result of the operation is also of that type. The implicit conversion is therefore always from the 'smaller' object to the 'larger'. The results of type conversion are summarised in table 6.1. An explicit type conversion can be obtained by using a 'cast'.

Table 6.1

| a | b | Result |
|---|---|---|
| char<br>short<br>int | char<br>short<br>int | int |
| char<br>short<br>int<br>long | long | long |
| char<br>short<br>int<br>long<br>unsigned long | unsigned long | unsigned long |
| char<br>short<br>int<br>long<br>float | float | float |
| char<br>short<br>int<br>long<br>float<br>double | double | double |
| char<br>short<br>int<br>long<br>float<br>double<br>long double | long double | long double |

The above rules have been defined by the C standard. Older, non-standard compilers will typically apply a different set of conversion rules. Most notably, many C compilers convert all floating point numbers to *double* before evaluating any floating point expressions.

## CAST

By prefixing an expression with one of the type names used earlier enclosed in parentheses, we force the expression to yield a result of the type indicated so that:

```
(long) 2 + 3
```

produces the result 5 which has type *long*. A cast can also be useful in forcing an argument to have the type of the corresponding parameter. The functions *exp*, *log*, and *sqrt*, which are to be found in the library of mathematical functions, expect a parameter of type *double*, and produce a result of type *double*. If we wish to obtain the natural logarithm of *x*, which has type *float*, then we can write:

```
log ((double) x)
```

If a function prototype is known before the call to it is encountered, the cast will be automatically performed. In this case, if the standard *math.h* header is included, the compiler will know to cast *x* to a value of type *double*. The assignment operator is treated in a different way to most of the other operators. The type of the expression of the right-hand side (rhs) is changed to the type of the identifier on the left-hand side. In appropriate circumstances, therefore, a rhs of type *double* is rounded to *float*, a rhs with type *float* is truncated to *int*, and an *int* is converted to *char* by ignoring excess high order bits. ANSI C standard guarantees that the rounding is performed accurately and truncation is always towards 0.

In the case of arithmetic constants, a result somewhat similar to casting can be achieved by specifying a type suffix. Type suffix is either an unsigned suffix, one of *U* or *u*, or a long suffix, one of *L* or *l*. The suffixes convert the constants to either *unsigned*, *long* or *unsigned long* values.

```
a = 123L;   /* a value of (long)123          */
b = 123U;   /* a value of (unsigned)123      */
c = 123ul;  /* a value of (unsigned long)123 */
d = 123Lu;  /* neither order nor case of
               the suffixes matters          */
```

## ASSIGNMENT OPERATORS

We have introduced a limited number of these operators at suitable places in the text. For example, the operator += was used to enable us to write:

```
sum += i;
```

rather than:

```
sum = sum + i;
```

An assignment in C is treated like any other operator in that, having made the assignment the value assigned is available for other use. Thus:

```
(sum += i) > max
```

adds *i* to *sum* and compares the assigned value with *max*. The validity of a 'multiple assignment' should therefore be apparent.

```
sum = total = start = 0;
```

The full list of assignment operators is:

```
+=            -=
*=            /=
%=            >>=
<<=           &=
^=            |=
```

The meanings of the various assignments will become obvious as we consider the different groups of operators.


## ARITHMETIC OPERATORS

We will introduce operators in the various groups by using them in simple expressions. While this may not be strictly necessary for the more familiar operators, it should help to clarify the action of the less familiar ones.

```
    + 5      5    unary plus
    - 5     -5    unary minus
7 + 5       12    add
7 - 5        2    subtract
7 * 5       35    multiply
7 / 5        1    divide
7 % 5        2    modulus
```

The type of the result of such expressions will be determined by the conversion rules given earlier. In the examples above, all results are of type *int*. When two items of type *int* are divided, the fractional part of the result is truncated to produce a result of type *int*. The modulus operator produces the remainder after division of one integral type by another. The result is of type *int*. Operands of type *double* or *float* may not be used with this operator.

A small example which uses most of the operators above is a function to evaluate Zeller's Congruence (Uspensky and Heaslet, 1939), shown in example 6.1. This function, when given a day, month and year (full form), produces a result in the range 0 to 6. With Sunday as day 0, this number represents the day of the week on which the given date fell. It can be used, for example, for calculating the day on which you were born.

*Example 6.1*

```
/* zeller returns a number in the range  */
/* 0..6 representing the day of the week */
/* on which the given date falls         */
/* Sunday is day 0                        */

int
zeller (int day, int month, int year)
{
    int temp, yr1, yr2;

    if (month < 3) { month += 10; year -= 1; }
    else month -= 2;

    yr1 = year / 100; yr2 = year % 100;
    temp = (26 * month - 1) / 10;

    return ((day + temp + yr2 + yr2/4 + yr1/4
                        - 2*yr1 + 49) % 7);
}

[ style 65.6 ]
```

## BITWISE OPERATORS

C enjoys well-deserved popularity as an 'implementation' language. This is in large measure due to the ease with which the user can access and manipulate bit patterns in memory. The following operators are available:

```
7 << 5    224(0xE0)   left shift
7 >> 5    0           right shift (beware sign propagation)
7 |  5    7           inclusive or
7 ^  5    2           exclusive or
7 &  5    5           and
  ~ 05    0177772     one's complement
```

Note the use of hexadecimal and octal constants above - hexadecimal constants are written with a leading *0x* or *0X*, and may use digits *0* through *9* and letters *A* through *F* (or *a* through *f*); octal constants are written with a leading *0*, and may use digits *0* through *7*. The last example, of the one's complement operator, assumes that the length of an *int* is 16 bits.

Bit manipulation, usually the preserve of assembly language programmers, is necessary, for example, when checking the bits of a status register and in masking data to be received or transmitted. An example to illustrate use of the operators need not be drawn from such a machine specific area. The 'feedback shift register' technique for generating pseudo-random numbers is easily expressed using the bitwise operators as example 6.2 shows.

*Example 6.2*

```
#include <limits.h>
#define PSHIFT 4
#define QSHIFT 11

int
random (int range)
{
    static int n = 1;

    n = n ^ n >> PSHIFT;
    n = (n ^ n << QSHIFT) & INT_MAX;
    return (n % (range+1));
}

/* the function is dependent upon */
/* the word length of the host    */
/* machine. The seed 'n' should   */
/* be capable of easier change    */
/* than is possible here.         */

[ style 75.5 ]
```

The standard header file *limits.h* defines the value for *INT_MAX* which is the maximum allowable value for an object of type *int*. If your compiler does not conform to the standard, and integers are two bytes long, you may have to define *INT_MAX* in the following way

```
#define INT_MAX 32767
```

The rationale behind this algorithm, which is a good source of random numbers, is given in Lewis (1975). A Pascal version, which makes an interesting comparison, is given in Meekings (1978). Remember too that since C makes it easy to print the value of a variable in either octal or hexadecimal, the results of bitwise operations can usually be displayed in an easily assimilated form.

## LOGICAL OPERATORS

These operators are usually used to combine one or more comparisons in the controlling expressions of conditional statements, *while* statements, and the other loop constructs.

| Example | | Result | Operation |
|---|---|---|---|
| 7 && 5 | | 1 | logical and |
| 7 \|\| 0 | | 1 | logical or |
| ! 0 | | 1 | logical not |

The important point that distinguishes these operators from the bitwise operators is that any non-zero operand is treated as 1 (*true*). A zero operand is treated as *false*. The result of the operation is 0 or 1 according to the normal rules for logical connectives. Expressions using && and || are evaluated left to right and evaluation should terminate once the truth or falsity of the expression is determined. For illustrative purposes, imagine that we wish to compute the mean rainfall given the total rainfall *train* over a number of days *days*. We might write:

```
if (days > 0)
    if ((mean = train / days) > 5.0) print ("%d\n", mean);
```

assuming that we wished to avoid division by zero. But consider:

```
if ((days > 0 && ((mean = train / days) > 5.0))
```

as an alternative test. It is only a useful alternative if, when *days* is zero, the expression in which *days* is a divisor is not evaluated. C guarantees that when the truth or falsity of an expression is known, as it is above when *(days > 0)* evaluates to zero (*false*), evaluation of the expression immediately terminates.

## RELATIONAL OPERATORS

Examples of some of these operators have appeared at several places in the text so far. The operators are:

```
>       greater than
>=      greater than or equal to
==      equal
!=      not equal
<=      less than or equal
<       less than
```

The test for a digit is a simple example of the use of two relational operators and a logical operator:

```
digit = (ch >= '0') && (ch <= '9');
```

## INCREMENT AND DECREMENT

The usefulness of the increment operator should by now have become apparent. The decrement operator is used in an entirely similar fashion, so that:

```
countdown--;
```

decrements countdown by one. What has not been emphasised so far is that both the increment operator and the decrement operator may be used either as a prefix or postfix to an operand. We may therefore write:

```
++count;              --countdown;
```

Such simple usage as this does not make clear what difference there might be between the prefixed or postfixed operator. The difference can be illustrated by the following example

```
up = 0;
printf ("%2d\n", up++); /* prints 0 */
printf ("%2d\n", ++up); /* prints 2 */
```

The first statement after the initialisation will print zero and then increment *up*. In the second print statement the value of *up* will be incremented (to two) and then printed. The prefixed form means increment (or decrement) and use, while the postfixed form means use and then increment (or decrement). The difference is important, as we will see, when dealing with array subscripts.

## CONDITIONAL OPERATOR

The conditional operator affords an easy and compact way to express a value which depends on a test. In the following example, the absolute value of *x* is computed.

```
if (x < 0)
    xabs = -x;
else
    xabs = x;
```

C gives us a more concise way to write such things, so their meaning becomes more apparent. The conditional operator takes three expressions and is used in the following format:

```
expression-1 ? expression-2 : expression-3
```

Expression-1 is evaluated and then tested. Based upon the results of this test, either one (but not both) of expression-2 and expression-3 will then be evaluated and that value will become the result of the whole conditional expression. If the value of expression-1 is true (non-zero), expression-2 is evaluated; otherwise, expression-3 is evaluated. Thus, we can write the absolute value computation as

```
xabs = (x < 0) ? -x : x;
```

Printing a heading only after a certain number of lines suddenly becomes easy to write

```
#define HEADING      "\n\n\n    - Treasure Island -\n\n\n"

printf ("%s", (no_lines % 60 == 0) ? HEADING : "");
```

Standard conversion rules will be used to bring the constituent values of the conditional expression to a common type to produce the result. So, in the following example, if $x$ is of type float when it is substituted by the pre-processor, the resulting type of the whole conditional expression is a float.

```
#define min_1(x)    (x < 1 ? x : 1)
```

## COMMA OPERATOR

The comma operator is syntactic sugar: it need not be provided since there are other facilities in the C language which can accomplish the same function; its use is more a question of style than of functionality. Expressions connected by a comma operator are executed in sequence. One use might be to initialise several quantities in a *for* statement. The following code might be used to scramble the letters in a word five successive times:

```
for (count = 0, j = word; count++ < 5; j = scramble (j))
    ;
```

First the expression on the left of the comma is evaluated and the result discarded; then the expression on the right of the comma is evaluated and used as the resulting value. The type of the result is the type of the operand on the right of the comma.

Ambiguity can arise in the cases where the comma can also be interpreted as a character separating items in a list (that is, arguments and initialisers). In those circumstances, the comma operator can only be used inside parentheses:

```
my_func (arg1, (c = C_INIT, (c + 1)*10), arg3);
```

## PRECEDENCE OF OPERATORS

Whatever programming language you use it is important to write expressions in a way that makes sense to you, the writer. (Bear in mind too that others will wish to read and understand your program.) In order to do this, and still produce programs that are syntactically and logically correct, it is necessary to understand how expressions are written and how they are interpreted. Operands must be separated by operators, and evaluation usually proceeds from left to right. Thus, in an expression such as:

```
a + b * c
```

it can be seen that the operators separate the operands, but we are accustomed to the multiplication of *b* and *c* being carried out before the addition of *a*. Formally we say that multiplication has a higher priority or precedence than addition. Parentheses can always be used to enforce the required priority. In C, however, there are occasions on which even this rule may not be as easy to apply as we would wish. Another possible source of confusion is that some operators, for example * and &, have more than one role. Consider for example:

```
*pint++
```

which is not part of a multiplication. It might mean increment the pointer (address) *pint* by one and retrieve the contents, or it might mean that the value *\*pint* is to be increased by one. In fact unary operators are evaluated from right to left and so the expression increments the pointer *pint* and not what it points to. The latter effect is achieved by:

```
(*pint)++
```

It is therefore important to know the order of precedence of operators and the direction of association. A table of this information is given in table 6.2. Operators are listed in decreasing priority, with operators in the same section having equal priority.

In the case of multiple operators of the same precedence and order of evaluation, for example in:

```
a + (b + c)
```

the compiler is free to rearrange the order of evaluation even in the presence of parenthesis. The above expression, while being evaluated, may thus become:

```
(a + b) + c
```

or even:

```
(a + c) + b
```

The order of evaluation of such expressions is immaterial under most normal circumstances. There are cases, however, in which it is important to group such expressions in order to avoid subtle rounding errors introduced by conversions. ANSI C provides a unary '+' operator for that purpose. The expression

```
a + +(b + c)
```

guarantees that *(b + c)* is evaluated first and the result is added to *a*.

Table 6.2

| Operator | Name | Associativity |
|----------|------|---------------|
| ( ) | parentheses | left to right |
| [ ] | brackets | |
| → | pointer | |
| . | dot | |
| | | |
| ++ | increment | right to left |
| - - | decrement | |
| (type) | cast | |
| * | contents of | |
| & | address of | |
| - | unary minus | |
| ~ | one's complement | |
| ! | logical NOT | |
| sizeof | size of | |
| | | |
| * | multiply | left to right |
| / | divide | |
| % | modulus | |
| | | |
| + | plus | left to right |
| - | minus | |
| | | |
| >> | shift right | left to right |
| << | shift left | |
| | | |
| > | greater than | left to right |
| >= | greater than or equal | |
| <= | less than or equal | |
| < | less than | |

| | | |
|---|---|---|
| == | equal | left to right |
| != | not equal | |
| & | bitwise AND | left to right |
| ^ | bitwise exclusive OR | left to right |
| \| | bitwise inclusive OR | left to right |
| && | logical AND | left to right |
| \|\| | logical OR | left to right |
| ?: | conditional | right to left |
| = | equals | right to left |
| += | plus equals | |
| -= | minus equals | |
| *= | multiply equals | |
| /= | divide equals | |
| %= | modulus equals | |
| >>= | shift right equals | |
| <<= | shift left equals | |
| &= | and equals | |
| ^= | exclusive or equals | |
| \|= | inclusive or equals | |

## SUMMARY

C has a well-deserved popularity among high-level and low-level programmers alike. Such popularity is, in large part, attributable to the richness of its set of operators, which allows a clear and natural expression of the program logic, with the additional bonus of an efficient translation into the underlying machine instructions. It is the large variety of operators that characterise the language, and possibly pose the greatest hurdle for the novice C programmer.

Time spent initially in learning how to use the full set of operators will be amply rewarded by clear, concise and efficient programs.

# 7 Arrays

In the examples used so far each data item that we wished to manipulate has been given a name, or identifier. Each identifier has associated with it a type, and a storage class. This association is made explicit through the declaration. But so far any identifier has represented a numeric value of one type or another, or a character. Consider again example 4.3 in which we produced a grade for a given mark. If we now change the specification of the problem, to ask that we produce the number of times that each grade was achieved, the statements in example 7.1 could appear in a suitable loop.

*Example 7.1*

```
/* assume a=b=c=d=e=f=0; prior to loop entry */

switch (mark / 20) {
    case  0: e++; break;
    case  1: d++; break;
    case  2: c++; break;
    case  3: b++; break;
    case  4: a++; break;
    default: f++;
}
```

While we can contemplate writing this when only five grades are involved, we would, if twenty-five grades were involved, look for a 'better way'.

## ARRAY DECLARATIONS

Instead of having individual identifiers for each grade total, which causes difficulty when dealing with them collectively, what would be much more useful would be a collective name for the grade totals together with a method of accessing each grade total. A street name is a collective name for several houses. The house number uniquely identifies each house of the street. An array name is a collective name for several data items of the same type. Each item has a unique reference number known as an index or subscript. If *grades* is the collective name for the five grade totals it could be declared as:

```
int grades[5];
```

In C array subscripts start at zero. The five grades can therefore be referred to as:

```
grades[0], grades[1], grades[2], grades[3], grades[4]
```

## POINTERS AND ARRAYS

Another method of referring to the individual elements of an array is available to us in C. The array name, *grades* in this case, is always treated as a pointer, or address. It points to the first element of the array. If, for example, we make a copy of the pointer, then we can increment and decrement the pointer value in order to refer to different elements of the array. Consider example 7.2.

*Example 7.2*

```
int grades[5], *gptr;

gptr = grades;    /* gptr points to grades[0] */
gptr++;           /* gptr points to grades[1] */
gptr++;           /* gptr points to grades[2] */
```

A subscript within square brackets is the more usual way to refer to elements within an array. Use of a pointer, while initially not so familiar, can become more convenient and is usually more economical in implementations of C. We shall move towards use of pointers for array access.

With an array to help us, we can now write example 7.1 in the following way:

```
int grades[5], *gptr, s, mark;

/* initialise array elements */

gptr = grades;
for (s = 0; s < 5; s++) *gptr++ = 0;

/* assume a function 'getmark' which */
/* returns either the next mark or   */
/* -1 to indicate the end            */

while ((mark = getmark ()) != -1) {
    s = mark / 20;
    if ((s >= 0) && (s < 5) ) grades[s]++;
}
```

There are several points of interest in this example. First note that the explicit constant 5, the number of elements in the array, appears three times in the program text. A symbolic name should be 'defined' to have this value, thus making a change in array size easy to accommodate. Secondly, note that the array elements are zeroised using the pointer *gptr*, and finally note that the increment operator can be used on an array element just as on any other variable.

## ARRAYS OF MORE THAN ONE DIMENSION

C allows us to use arrays of more than one dimension. Imagine that instead of simply printing letters in a 7*5 grid, as we did in the early examples of chapter 2, we wish to store these representations of characters in a 7*5 array, that is, an array with 7 rows and 5 columns. If we wish to access these elements using a pointer, then it is essential to appreciate that in C arrays are stored by row.

first three rows of big I

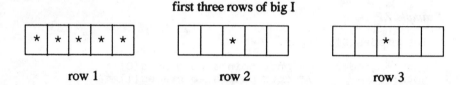

row 1                              row 2                              row 3

This means that the rightmost of the two subscripts changes more quickly because elements are accessed in the order that they are stored. A two-dimensional array can easily be visualised as a table, and therefore we shall initially use subscripts, rather than a pointer, to access the elements (example 7.3). We shall later rethink this approach.

*Example 7.3*

```
#define ROWMAX 7
#define COLMAX 5

char letter[ROWMAX][COLMAX];
int  col;

/* fill array with spaces */

for (row = 0; row < ROWMAX; row++)
    for (col = 0; col < COLMAX; col++)
        letter[row][col] = ' ';

/* alternatively we could write .. */

for (row = 0; row < ROWMAX; row++)
    for (col = 0; col < COLMAX; letter[row][col++] = ' ')
        ;
```

Observe that each subscript is enclosed by square brackets and that the final *for* statement does not have a statement to control. This is because each element of *letter* can be set to a space in such a way that the column subscript is incremented after it has been used to access the array element. This is an occasion where use of

```
++col
```

rather than

```
col++
```

would not have the required effect.

## ARRAYS AS PARAMETERS

Pursuing our example a little further, for those upper case letters of the alphabet that can be constructed from horizontal and vertical lines only, it would be convenient to have functions that fill a row, or a column, with a given character. The functions of example 7.4 fulfil this task.

*Example 7.4*

```
#define ROWMAX 7
#define COLMAX 5
void
fillrow (int row, char matrix[ROWMAX][COLMAX])
{
    int c;
    for (c = 0; c < COLMAX; matrix[row][c++] = '*')
        ;
}
void
fillcol (int col, char matrix[][COLMAX])
{
    int r;
    for (r = 0; r < ROWMAX; matrix[r++][col] = '*')
        ;
}
[ style 54.6 ]
```

Each of the functions must change the contents of the array and, as we saw in chapter 2, must therefore have access to the address of the data item to be changed. But since the array name is the address of the first element, it can be used without modification as a parameter to a function. The functions of example 7.4 will access the contents of the array that is the argument, and it should therefore be obvious that the purpose of the code

```
char matrix[ROWMAX][COLMAX];
```

in each function is simply to establish the type of the parameter 'matrix'. No storage allocation is performed. It may not be necessary, but it is not wrong, to give the size of each dimension. Given that arrays are stored in row-major order, the size in the first dimension may be omitted, as it has been in the function *fillcol* of example 7.4.

It should be apparent that the functions of 7.4 also make use of what we called implicit parameters in chapter 2. *fillrow* uses *COLMAX* which, although its definition is a *define* statement, could as easily have been, say, a static *const* variable of the file containing the functions. The functions are not 'self-contained' in the sense that the identifiers that they use do not all derive from either the parameter list or the local variable declarations. This is a common occurrence but worth emphasising. Assuming the definitions of 7.3 and 7.4 we can write:

```
void
makeH (char mat[ROWMAX][COLMAX])
{
    fillcol (0, mat);
    fillcol (COLMAX, mat);
    fillrow (3, mat);
}
```

and thereafter write:

```
makeH (letter_matrix);
```

## STRINGS

In the preceding section we used an array of characters and, because of the particular example chosen, all elements of the array were always used. But when we wish to deal with strings, which are stored as an array of characters, it is inefficient to assume that the string will occupy all elements of the array in which it is stored. We must expect that either the length of the string is stored along with it, or that the end of a string is denoted by a special character. C adopts the convention that the end of a string is denoted by the NULL character '\0'.

*Example 7.5*

```
#define WIDTH 80

char mess[WIDTH], *m;

mess[0] = 'h';
mess[1] = 'e';
mess[2] = 'l';
mess[3] = 'l';
mess[4] = 'o';
mess[5] = '\0';
```

The rather laboured statements of example 7.5 cause six characters to be stored in *mess*. Since the last character is NULL we can say that the array *mess* holds a string. The string may be printed by any of the following statements:

```
m = mess; while (*m != NULL) putchar (*m++);

while (((m - mess) < WIDTH) && (*m != NULL)) putchar (*m++);

printf ("%s", m);
```

The tedious parts of the above examples are those that deal with individual characters. While this may sometimes be necessary, we more usually wish to process the string as a whole. We have been accustomed to writing a string as a sequence of characters between double quotes thus

```
"C-ing is believing"
```

It is therefore not unreasonable to expect that we may assign a string to an identifier without the necessity of doing it character by character. We achieve this as follows

```
char *sptr;
sptr = "C-ing is believing";
```

From its declaration *sptr* is a pointer to a character. In particular, after assignment, *sptr* points to the first character of the string. It is important to note that the assignment does not copy the character string. The declaration of *sptr* offers no storage space for characters. The string is stored somewhere, we know not where, except that we have in *sptr* a pointer to the first character. This is usually sufficient. If, for some reason, it is necessary to copy the string into local storage, then this must be done with a function such as *strcpy* which copies a string from one storage place to another. In example 7.5 when storing one character at a time in *mess* we were responsible for ensuring that a NULL character followed the last useful character. When, as above, a string is assigned to a pointer, a NULL is automatically appended to the character sequence. Use of pointers to refer to a string is much the most common and convenient way of dealing with strings in C. Any functions provided by a C implementation to help process strings, compare strings, find the length of a string, find a character within a string, will require the user to pass pointers as parameters.

We have said so far that one dimensional arrays, such as character arrays in the previous examples, are often treated in a way similar to pointers. Whereas it is true in certain situations, such as parameter passing, we have to fully appreciate differences between pointers and one dimensional arrays. The array names, such as *mess* in Example 7.5, contain an address of the first element of the array. In that sense they are just as pointers and can be used as such in parameters to functions. However, declaration of an array reserves storage for all elements of the array and then places the address of the beginning of this storage in the symbol representing the array. References to particular elements of the array through the use of square brackets will calculate appropriate offsets from the beginning of the array's storage area. Declaration of pointers, on the other hand, does not reserve storage for any objects that the pointer may be pointing to. A pointer is simply a place to store an address of an object and does not represent any objects unless assigned a particular address during execution of a program. The following example may clarify some of these points.

*Example 7.6*

```
#define WIDTH 80

void
example (void)
{
    char *m, mess[WIDTH], ch;
    char str[WIDTH] = "forty two";
                    /* initialisation is allowed */

    /* Note that the initialisation above is treated
       by the C compiler as a copy operation.
       Thus, the string "forty two" is copied into
       storage allocated for str. Compare with the
       first statement below. */

    mess = "ZX";    /* WRONG: mess has storage already
                       allocated to it, namely
                       the mess array. You cannot
                       change it; mess is really a
                       constant pointing to the array
                       storage. Only the content of
                       the storage can be changed,
                       not its address */
    mess[0] = 'Z'; /* OK: first element of the array
                       is now 'Z' */
    mess[1] = 'X'; /* OK: second element of the array
                       is now 'X' */
    *m = ch;        /* WRONG: m does not point to
                       anything yet */
    ch = *m;        /* WRONG: m does not point to
                       anything yet */
    m = "Message"; /* OK: m is assigned the address
                       of the string */
    ch = *m;        /* OK; ch now contains the first
                       character of the string, 'M' */
    ch = *(m+2);    /* OK: ch now contains the third
                       character of the string, 's' */
    m = mess;       /* OK: m is assigned the address
                       stored in mess, that is, the
                       address of the first element
                       of the mess array */
    ch = *m;        /* OK: ch now contains the first
                       character of mess, 'Z' */

    return;
}
```

## ARRAYS OF POINTERS

A program that was designed to report a variety of error messages to its user might use the approach given in example 7.7.

*Example 7.7*

```
char *error[30];

/* error is an array of 30 pointers to char */

error[0] = "not enough arguments";
error[1] = "too many arguments";
error[2] = "invalid arguments";

/* etc., etc. */

/* to report error number 'i' */

printf ("*** %s ***\n", error[i]);
```

The patterns of asterisks held in 7*5 arrays of characters, while not especially useful, are easily visualised. Imagine therefore, that we wish to construct, and store in this form, representations of all upper case letters of the alphabet. If *lptr[i-1]* is to point to the representation of the *i*th letter, then we need the declaration:

```
char (*lptr[26])[7][5];
```

This declaration says that *lptr* is a 26 element array of pointers. The pointers point to 7*5 arrays of characters. If we wish to associate the eighth pointer with the eighth letter of the alphabet, H, we could do this easily by the statement:

```
makeH (lptr[7]);
```

The preceding examples should have helped to clarify the way in which two-dimensional arrays can be used in C. But a moment's reflection will reveal that in order to store our upper case characters in this manner we would need storage space for 26*7*5 characters. Furthermore, each character needs to be placed in the correct element. This is certainly not making the best use of the facilities available in C. Even in our earliest examples we recognised that it was worth having functions or *define* statements to deal with five stars, a middle star, and two end stars (example 2.3). Following this course we could set up strings as follows:

```
char *allstars, *endstars, *midstars;

allstars = "*****";
endstars = "*   *";
midstars = "  *  ";
```

An array of seven elements, where each element is a pointer such as *allstars*, can now be used to represent a character composed of asterisks. Thus the character H can now be represented by seven pointers, six of which point to the same object.

```
void
makeH (char *sptr[ROWMAX])
{
    sptr++ = sptr++ = sptr++ = endstars;
    sptr++ = allstars;
    sptr++ = sptr++ = sptr = endstars;
}
```

We now need an array of 26 pointers in which each pointer points to an array of seven pointers which point to strings. This is obtained with the declaration:

```
char (*lptr[ROWMAX])[26];
```

The call to our new version of *makeH* defined above would be:

```
makeH (lptr[7]);
```

The advantage of rethinking our example, or rather the way to express it in C, has been that we have eliminated the need to assign characters to individual array elements. We now assign strings to pointers. Further, our storage requirement is considerably reduced as we store only one copy of each string (row) of characters. Each 'big' character can be represented by seven pointers and we need twenty-six such characters. We therefore save ourselves writing effort, storage space, and run time, by thinking about our task in a way which enables us to take full advantage of the facilities offered by C.

It is important, and useful, to be thoroughly familiar with the handling of strings and pointers in C. The next example, which is complete, should help to consolidate the work on strings.

*Example 7.8*

```
/* Soundex code generator: to transform a string */
/* into a code that tends to bring together all  */
/* variants of the same name (usually surname)   */
/*      -  (Knuth, 1973)                          */

#include <stdio.h>

void encode (char *s);
void dumpdups (const char *s);
void dumpzeros (const char *s);
void fixup (char *s);

int
main (void)
{
```

```
    char str[20];

    printf ("\nCharacter string ?");  /* ask user..      */
    scanf ("%s", str);                /* for a string    */

    encode (str);                          /* encode all but  */
                                           /* the first char  */
    dumpdups (str);                        /* erase adjacent  */
                                           /* duplicate codes */

    dumpzeros (str);                       /* erase zero codes*/

    fixup (str);                           /* pad or truncate */
                                           /* to four digits  */

    printf ("\nSoundex code is : %s\n", str);
                                           /* tell user*/
    return(0);
}

void
encode (char *s)
{
    static char code[] = "01230120022455012623010202";

    while (*++s)
        *s = code[*s - 'a'];
}
void
dumpdups (const char *s)
{
    char *t;

    while (*s)
        if (*s == *(s+1)) {
            t = s + 1;
            while (*t = *(t+1))
                t++;
        } else s++;
}

void
dumpzeros (const char *s)
{
    char *t;

    while (*s)
        if (*s == '0') {
            t = s;
            while (*t = *(t+1))
                t++;
        } else s++;
}
```

```
void
fixup (char *s)
{
    int i;

    for (i = 1; *++s && i < 4; i++)
        ;
    for ( ; i < 4; i++)
        *s++ = '0';
    *s = (char)0;
}
```

[ style 73.9 ]

In example 7.8 only one copy of the string exists. The functions are given a pointer to this copy and may modify the string. The string is obtained from a call to *scanf* which we have not so far used in the examples on strings. Note that *encode* initialises the array *code* at its declaration with one digit for each letter of the alphabet. Both *dumpdups* and *dumpzeros* use the expression $*t = *(t+1)$ in a *while* statement to eliminate adjacent identical characters, while *fixup* capitalises upon the flexibility of the *for* statement.


SUMMARY

The availability of arrays has clearly made a significant difference to the ease with which we can express our tasks in C. Pointers, together with arrays, provide us with easy-to-use and economical programming aids. C does not limit us to arrays as a way of storing data items with a collective name. We are also able to use structures, which enable us to group together data items of differing types - this is the subject of the next chapter. Pointers too have a wider role to play than we have thus far indicated, and we will return to them in a later chapter.

The elements of C that we have covered so far constitute a 'basic set'. It is perfectly possible to write meaningful C programs armed with only that knowledge. The remaining chapters deal with more advanced topics, without which your C armoury would be incomplete.

# 8 More Data Types

In our discussion so far, all data types of identifiers have been simple: they consist of one elementary type. The elementary types are:

| | |
|---|---|
| (char) | characters |
| (int) | integers |
| (float) | floating point |

Chars and ints can be either signed or unsigned, and ints and floats can have modifiers short or long. A "long float" is referred to as a "double." Unless otherwise explicitly stated in a declaration, the default type is int.

If these were the only data types the C language could represent, many problemswould be much more difficult to express than they should be. Part of the great flexibility of C is that the language provides a way to combine elementary types into new derived types called structures and unions.

## STRUCTURES AND UNIONS

When we combine types, we can do it in one of two ways: we can either lay them end to end so that none of them overlap and each of them contains independent values, or we can overlay them on top of each other, so that they all start at the same machine storage location and overlap.

If we lay the types next to each other so that none of them overlap, we create a structure, a type which is the concatenation of the individual member elementary types. Each of the variables starts at a different storage location, one after the other in a series. Therefore, the length of a structure is at least as much as the sum of the lengths of its members. Some compilers insert space in between members of a structure in order to enforce data type address alignment restrictions of the hardware. As a result, the length of a structure may be more than the sum of the lengths of its members because of "holes" in the structure form.

If we overlay types on top of each other, we create a union, a type which is the union of the individual member elementary types. The same memory storage area is accessed by all of the variables within the union, and it is up to the application to know which particular data type occupies the space at any given time. Since each of the variables starts at the same location, the length of the union is the length of the longest member.

Pictorially, we can represent the distinction between structures and unions as:

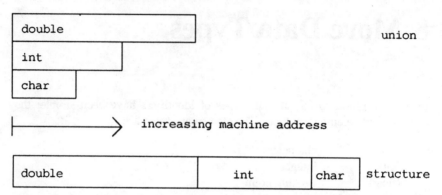

If we assume that the size of a char is 1 byte, of an int is 2 bytes, and of a double, 4 bytes, then the size of the union is 4 bytes, while the size of the structure is 7 bytes.

Structures are used to group together related data so that they become more manageable. Consider, as an example, a date. We can represent the date by three numbers: the month of the year, the day of the month, and the year. By grouping these together, we can create a new type:

```
struct date_type {
    short int month;  /* Month of year - 1 --> 12 */
    short int day;    /* Day of month - 1 --> 31  */
    short int year;   /* Year                     */
};
```

The above statement declares a derived type (struct date_type) and its form, i.e., what its members are. The identifier date_type is called the structure tag or template name; the compiler will know what a *struct date_type* is at any point after this declaration.

No storage is allocated by the above statement, however. The template name before the left curly bracket is used only to identify the form of the structure so that it can be referenced more easily afterward. The name of the template is called a tag. To create an instance of this new type at the time of creation of the tag, an identifier is placed after the right curly bracket:

```
struct date_type {
    short int month;
    short int day;
    short int year;
} birth;                        /* Date of birth */
```

If the tag has been previously defined, it is sufficient to just specify its name without repeating the definition of its type:

```
struct date_type birth;         /* Date of birth */
```

Structures and unions nest; that is, they can be embedded within other structures and unions. Arrays can be put inside structures or unions, also. So, if we were interested in storing information about a person, we might create a structure:

```
struct person_type {
    char name[NAMESIZE];      /* Name of person */
    struct date_type birth;   /* Date of birth  */
    struct date_type death;   /* Date of death  */
};
```

We can even create arrays of structures, so that this information about everyone in a group could be stored by declaring:

```
struct person_type brits[UK_POPULATION];
```

Unions of all types can be created in a similar fashion. This facility to group data into a new type makes it easier to manage, and thus reduces the complexity of the programming task.

As an example of a union, consider a piece of storage which will sometimes hold an int, and at other times a double. The declaration for such a union would be written:

```
union int_double {
    int i;
    double d;
};
```

## ACCESSING STRUCTURES AND UNIONS

Only a limited number of operations can be performed on structures and unions. It obviously does not make sense to, for example, add or multiply structures, but it is essential to be able to access their members. Several structure and union operations are available: a member can be accessed, the address can be taken with the & operator, structures can be assigned values *en masse* by copying elements from one structure to another of the same type, and they can be used as parameters to, and return values from functions. For the previously declared structure *birth*,

```
birth.day
```

represents the member identified by *day*, and

```
&birth
```

represents the address of that structure. If *pbirth* is declared as a pointer to a *date_type* structure and then initialised:

```
struct date_type *pbirth = &birth;
```

then the *day* member from such a   pointer is accessed with the pointer operator:

```
pbirth->day
```

When accessing a member of a structure directly, the dot operator is used; for indirect access from a pointer to a structure, the pointer operator is used.
The name of the person in the first element of the array of structures *brits* declared above is accessed:

```
brits[0].name
```

which is an array of characters holding the person's name. Note that this is distinct from the first character of the name, which would be accessed as:

```
brits[0].name[0]
```

The assignment operator can be used to initialise all elements of one structure with the corresponding values from another structure.  Both source and target structures must be of exactly the same type as in

```
struct date_type birth, death;

birth = death;
```

To give a structure initial values at compile time, an initialiser similar to the one used for character arrays can be specified in a declaration like this:

```
struct person_type henry_viii = {
    "Henry VIII",           /* Name                        */
    { 6, 28, 1491 },        /* Born June 28, 1491     */
    { 1, 28, 1547 }         /* Died January 28, 1547 */
};
```

Using the dot and pointer operators to access members works with nested structures, so that

```
henry_viii.birth.year
```

would have the value 1491.

It should be noted that only conforming C implementations must support structure assignment by copying contents of each structure member, and allow structures to be passed to and returned from functions. Some of the old compilers may not fully implement structure and union operations as defined by the C standard. In particular, it may not be possible to pass structures as arguments to functions or copy the content of one structure into another structure of the same type simply by specifying the assignment operator. This limitation is more of an inconvenience than a real problem. One can always specify a set of assignment statements for each member of a structure, or pass an address of a structure to a function.

## ENUMERATIONS

Still another method for creating new types is available in the C language. In an enumerated type, a variable can assume one of a finite set of values which are listed at the place the type is declared. If we create a type to model the five flavours of ice cream available at a certain store, we could say:

```
enum flavour_type {
    CHOCOLATE,
    VANILLA,
    STRAWBERRY,
    COFFEE,
    RASPBERRY
};
```

Thereafter, a variable of type *flavour_type* can take on any of the values enumerated. The values are treated like constants and can be used anywhere constants can be used.

```
enum flavour_type flavour = CHOCOLATE;
```

would create a variable named *flavour*, and give it an initial value of *CHOCOLATE*. Please note, however, that no type checking in function calls or assignment statements is performed for *enum* variables. It is quite possible to assign a value of, say, 15 to a variable declared as *enum flavour_type*. All *enum* variables are really treated as integers.

In our previous example, we could modify the *person_type* structure to include information about the sex of a person. Since the sex of most people is only one of two possible values, we can define an enumerated type to represent it:

```
struct person_type {
    char name[NAMESIZE];        /* Name of person */
    enum sex_type {
        MALE,
        FEMALE
    } sex;                      /* Sex */
    struct date_type birth;     /* Date of birth */
    struct date_type death;     /* Date of death */
};
```

To demonstrate the use of *enum* types, we could write a routine which would recognise an argument of a string of characters as being either "MALE" or "FEMALE," and then return the appropriate *enum* value:

```
enum sex_type
get_sex (char *str)
{
    return (strcmp (str, "MALE") ? FEMALE : MALE);
}
```

The above routine uses the standard C library function strcmp, which compares two character arrays, and returns an integer which is less than, equal to, or greater than 0 depending on whether the first argument is lexicographically less than, equal to, or greater than the second.

## BIT FIELDS

There are times when it becomes necessary to pack several pieces of information into the storage that would normally be occupied by a single variable. Such circumstances can occur when manipulating huge amounts of data, or when dealing with boolean values or flags. For these occasions, C provides us with a way to indicate how many bits should be assigned for each variable. When we access one of these fields, the compiler will isolate the correct bits and allow us to manipulate the field as though it was stored as a separate variable. For example, if we wanted to save space and squeeze the date structure so it occupied as little machine storage as possible, we could define it as:

```
struct {
    unsigned month : 4;
    unsigned day : 5;
    unsigned year : 11;
} short_date;
```

Since the month of the year can only be a number between 1 and 12, we need only 4 bits to represent it; the day can only be between 1 and 31 (5 bits required), and we can let the year be represented by 11 bits (allows us up to the year 2047). Thus, *short_date* occupies only 20 bits, instead of the 48 bits it would take if the month, day, and year were each 16 bits (*int*).

There are some restrictions on the use of bit fields - there are no arrays of fields; and, because they might not begin on a byte or word boundary, they have no address, so the & operator cannot be applied to them.

As the cost of memory continues to decline, it seems that bit fields will be most useful in those cases when compact representation of data is paramount.

## VOID

An additional type, *void* is available to describe those objects which have no value. This is useful for declaring functions that return no value, or casting expressions which generate values that are to be discarded. As an example, the function *exit*, which does not return to the calling routine after it is invoked, could be declared:

```
void exit (int);
```

A void expression denotes a nonexistent value, and as such, can only be used as an expression statement, or as the left operand of a comma expression.

A pointer to *void* denotes a "generic" pointer. Such a pointer is an address of an object of an unspecified data type. It can be used in most expressions other pointers can be used in, but cannot be incremented or decremented. You will recall that the following expression:

```
long *ptr;
ptr++;
```

increments *ptr* such that it points to a next element of type *long*. Since *void \** may point to any data type, the increment size is unknown and thus the result of the increment operator is undefined. One of the conveniences of C used to be interchangeability of pointers and integer types. It afforded very easy pointer arithmetic and was useful in many low level applications. The C standard no longer guarantees that pointers will fit into storage allocated for integers. That is, on some hardware pointers may be larger than any integer type; hence, the pointer to *void* type which always guarantees to be large enough to accept an address of any object.

## TYPEDEF

In C, it is possible to use a shorthand notation to describe fundamental or derived types. A declaration using *typedef* defines synonyms for the indicated type. For example, we could define the *date_type* structure previously mentioned in this chapter as a *typedef* called *DATE* in the following manner:

```
typedef struct {
    short int month;    /* Month of year - 1 -> 12 */
    short int day;      /* Day of month - 1 -> 31 */
    short int year;     /* Year */
} DATE;
```

After this declaration, the compiler will understand the use of *DATE* as a reference to the above structure template. It is important to note that no new types are generated; the use of *typedef* is just a shorthand for an existing type. The semantics are exactly the same for typedef variables as for variables whose definitions are written out the long way. Typedefs can be used to declare synonyms for unions, enums, and fundamental data types in exactly the same way.

Arrays, functions, and pointers can be used in typedef declarations as well. The declaration

```
typedef int ARRAY_DATE[3];
```

allows the definition of a variable

```
ARRAY_DATE date;
```

which is an array of three *ints*. If we wanted to have a synonym for a pointer to a *DATE* structure, we could write:

```
typedef DATE *PDATE;
```

Thus, *PDATE* would be a pointer to a *DATE* structure.

*typedef* is especially useful for long and convoluted declarations. Such declarations may be expected in applications defining complicated data structures and providing functions operating on such data. The following few lines of a hypothetical program listing provide increasingly complex *typedef* specifications.

```
typedef int *int_ptr_t;
typedef int (*int_func_t)(int_ptr_t, int_ptr_t);
typedef int_func_t func_list_t[6];

int_ptr_t ptr;        /* ptr is a pointer to integer */
int_func_t func;      /* func is a pointer to function
                         returning int and accepting
                         two pointers to int */
func_list_t list;     /* list is an array of six
                         pointers to functions returning
                         int and accepting two pointers
                         to int */
int_ptr_t knot (func_list_t);
                      /* knot (Gordian?) is a function
                         accepting an array of six
                         pointers to functions returning
                         int and accepting two pointers
                         to int each; the function
                         returns one pointer to int */
```

## SUMMARY

The object of the game in programming is to reduce the complexity of problems to a form where the solution is readily understandable to both the writer and the reader. Derived data types afford us the luxury of defining arbitrarily complex aggregates so that we can group variables together in some logical fashion, where it is sensible to do so. This principle of data abstraction allows us to concentrate more on the fundamental ideas of the problem, rather than on the details of its implementation. Without derived data types, it would be impossible to implement the data structures that are required to solve complicated problems. The next chapter deals with the development of these data structures.

# 9 Pointers Revisited

Our use of pointers so far has been largely restricted to the processing of character strings. In this chapter we will explore much more imaginative uses of this very powerful feature of C. In particular, we will need pointers to simplify the handling of the data structures that are typical of more complex programs.

Choosing the right data structure to contain the data manipulated by a program is at least as important as choosing the right algorithm, and in many cases, a poor choice of data structure will lead to a clumsy program. Data structures and algorithms are intricately intertwined and a choice of one profoundly influences the other.

## POINTERS TO STRUCTURES

Given an array of structures of the kind

```
typedef struct {
    int a;
    char b;
    float c;
} STRUCT;

STRUCT array[10];
```

we have two methods of stepping through the array, examining the individual elements. One way we are already familiar with - using subscripts, so that *array[i]* refers to the *(i+1)*th element (because the first element is subscript 0). The other way is to use a pointer:

```
STRUCT *p;

for (i = 0, p = array; i < 10; i++, p++)
    printf ("array[%d] %d %c %f\n", i, p->a, p->b, p->c);
```

Note that when we say *i++* we mean "add 1 to *i*", but when we say *p++* we mean "add enough to *p* to make it point to the next element," and this is precisely what C does. Pointer arithmetic takes account of the underlying type, so that *p++* means something different if *p* is a pointer to *STRUCT* or *char* - in the latter case, since the underlying type is one byte, *p* is actually incremented by 1.

It is for this reason that the expressions *A[i]* and *\*(A+i)* are functionally equivalent, regardless of the type of *A*.

91

## ALLOCATION OF STORAGE

If we wanted to read lines of text from a file and store them internally for subsequent processing, one way that we could do it is to declare an array of fifty 132-character lines, and read the data into it. The problem with this is that we don't know how many lines there will be, or how long they are. As long as the lines are less than 132 characters, and as long as there are less than 50 lines, then the program will work, even though we may have reserved much more space than we actually need (suppose we only have two 10-character lines!). A closer look at memory allocation is definitely warranted.

Storage for identifiers can be allocated in several ways. When an identifier is defined with the storage class *static* or *extern*, the compiler allocates memory for this identifier once, and it exists for the life of the program. Identifiers defined with the storage class *automatic* have memory allocated for them when control enters the function that defines them, and deallocated or 'freed' when control exits that function. Thus, an *automatic* variable exists only when the function which defines it is executing. There are times when a programmer would like to allocate storage for a variable in one function, and have that variable exist until all processing related to it is complete, which may be long after the function which defined it has exited. In addition, the programmer may not even know how much storage will be required, as in our case. To provide the programmer with complete flexibility, the *malloc* and *free* functions can be used to perform dynamic memory allocation.

The *malloc* library routine is a general purpose memory allocator; its argument is the size (in bytes) of the memory desired. If successful, the return value is a pointer to a block of memory of the requested size. When the block is no longer needed, the *free* routine can be called with the pointer to the block to be freed as its argument.

Using these facilities, we can now manage memory more efficiently, and eliminate the restriction on the number of lines that can be read in, as shown in example 9.1.

*Example 9.1*

```
#include <stdlib.h>
#include <stdio.h>

/* Maximum length of input line */

#define LINESIZE 132

/* Error handling macro */
#define ERROR(msg) {fprintf (stderr, "%s\n", msg); exit(1);}

/* Linked list structure */
```

```
typedef struct list {
    char text[LINESIZE];
    struct list *next;
} LIST;

LIST *lines = NULL,      /* Pointer to head of the list */
     *this_line = NULL,  /* Pointer to current element */
     *new_line;          /* Pointer to a new element */

int eof = 0;             /* End of file flag */

while (!eof) {
    /* Allocate space for a new line */

    if (!(new_line = (LIST *) malloc (sizeof(LIST))))
        ERROR("Memory exhausted");

    /* Initialise next pointer */

    new_line->next = (LIST *) NULL;

    /* Read in the next line */

    if (!gets (new_line->text))
        eof = 1;
    else
        /* If this is the first line, set head
           and current pointer to it */

        if (!lines)
            lines = this_line = new_line;

        /* Otherwise, link current line to new
           one and advance current line */

        else
            this_line = this_line->next = new_line;
}
```

[ style 53.0 ]

Here we have generated a "linked list" data structure, where each element in the structure, as well as containing the data, has a pointer to the next element in the list. Thus, we finish up with exactly as many elements as there are lines in the input - no more, no less. We could print out the text afterwards by

```
for (this_line = lines; this_line;
                        this_line = this_line->next)
    printf ("%s\n", this_line->text);
```

When allocating space dynamically in this way, it is important to remember that we need to de-allocate, or free, the space at some time. This will be done automatically when the program exits, but if space limitations require that you free the space before then (if, for example, you wish to re-use the space for other purposes), it can be freed by

```
#include <stdlib.h>

LIST *next_line;

while (lines) {
    next_line = lines->next;
    free (lines);
    lines = next_line;
}
```

and this will leave the variable *lines* set to a NULL value, so that, if used inadvertently, it will not pick up garbage data.

Of course, we have still potentially allocated more space than we need, since each line reserves 132 characters, regardless of its actual length. A better structure would be one that looked like

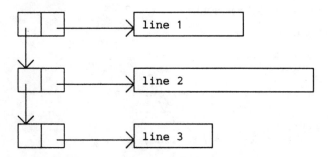

which would be declared as

```
typedef struct list {
    char *text;
    struct list *next;
} LIST;
```

and we would have to allocate storage for both the list element and for the data, as shown in example 9.2.

*Example 9.2*

```
#include <stdlib.h>
#include <stdio.h>

/* Maximum line size */

#define BUFSIZE 2048

char data[BUFSIZE];

while (!eof) {
    if (!(new_line = (LIST *) malloc (sizeof(LIST))))
        ERROR("Memory exhausted");

    new_line->next = (LIST *) NULL;
```

```
    if (!gets (data))
        eof = 1;
    else {
        /* Allocate enough space for this line */

        if (!(new_line->text =
                    (char *) malloc (strlen(data)+1)))
            ERROR("Memory exhausted");

        /* Copy the line read in */

        strcpy (new_line->text, data);

        if (!lines)
            lines = this_line = new_line;
        else
            this_line = this_line->next = new_line;
    }
}

[ style 55.5 ]
```

Now we are allocating exactly the amount of storage required. Note also that the limit on line length is only that it be less than 2048 characters!

## COMPLEX DATA STRUCTURES

As an example of a more complex data structure, consider the program of example 9.3, together with its header file in example 9.4. This program constructs a family tree from input data, and prints out the pedigree chart of a named individual.

The principal data structure is an array of elements of type *PERSON*, which looks like

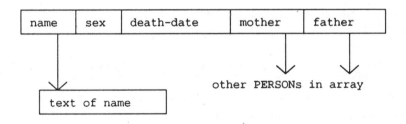

The dates of birth and death are themselves structures, nested within the *PERSON* structure.

*Example 9.3*

```c
#include "family.h"
#include <ctype.h>

/* Maximum number of people in input data */

#define MAXPEOPLE 64

/* Array for data structure */

static PERSON people[MAXPEOPLE+1];

/* Pointer to output image area */
static char *space;

/* Months of year */

static char *month[MONTHS] =
    { "JAN",    "FEB",    "MAR",    "APR",
      "MAY",    "JUN",    "JUL",    "AUG",
      "SEP",    "OCT",    "NOV",    "DEC" };

/* Global variables */

static int curr_level = 0;
static int max_level = 0;
static int totrows, totcols;

int
main (int argc, char *argv[])
{
    char line[LINESIZE];   /* Input line */
    register int i;        /* General purpose counter */
    register PERSON *p;    /* Pointer to data structure */

    /* Arguments can be passed in on the command line as :
                command arg1 arg2 ...
       where argc is the argument count (including the
       command name), and argv[i] are the arguments
       (argv[0] is the command itself, argv[1] is the
       first argument, etc.) */

    if (argc != 2)
        ERROR("Usage: ftree <name>", "");

    /* Initialise the data structure */

    for (i = 0; i <= MAXPEOPLE; people[i++].name = NULL)
        ;

    /* Input lines consist of fields separated by "tokens"
       from SEPSTRING. Read in each line, extracting the
       fields and entering them into the data structure.
       Ignore lines beginning with "*" (comments). */

    while (gets (line) && strlen(line)) {
        if (line[0] == '*')
            continue;
        p = get_name (strtok (line, SEPSTRING));
        p->sex = get_sex (strtok (NULL, SEPSTRING));
        p->birth = get_date (strtok (NULL, SEPSTRING));
        p->death = get_date (strtok (NULL, SEPSTRING));
        p->father = get_name (strtok (NULL, SEPSTRING));
        p->mother = get_name (strtok (NULL, SEPSTRING));
    }
```

```
        /* Find out how big the tree will be .. */

        get_level (p = get_name (argv[1]));
        totrows = (5 * power (2, max_level) - 1);
        totcols = (max_level + 1) * COLPLEV;

        /* ... and allocate space for the output */

        if (!(space = malloc ((unsigned) (totrows * totcols))))
            ERROR("Memory exhausted", "");

        /* Initialise the output area with spaces using
           the library function memset */

        memset (space, (int) ' ', totrows * totcols);

        /* Generate the output image ... */

        drawtree (p, 0, 1);
        vlines ();

        /* ... print it ... */

        printtree ();

        /* ... and exit */

        return (0);
}

/**
 *  Find the person indicated by the supplied name
 *  in the 'people' array. If the person is currently
 *  non-existent, insert them into the array. Return
 *  a pointer to the person if successful, otherwise
 *  terminate with an error message.
 **/

PERSON *
get_name (const char *str)
{
        register PERSON *p;        /* Data strucure pointer */
        static DATE zero_date = { 0, 0, 0 }; /* Date */
        /* '-' means unknown */

        if (!strcmp (str, "-"))
            return (PERSON *) 0;
        /* Search the array for a matching name */

        for (p = people; p->name && strcmp (p->name, str); p++)
            ;

        /* If found, return the pointer ... */

        if (p->name)
            return p;

        /* ... otherwise make sure there's enough room ... */

        if (p >= &people[MAXPEOPLE])
            ERROR("Too many people", "");

        /* ... add them to the end ... */

        if (!(p->name = malloc ((unsigned) strlen (str) + 1)))
            ERROR("Memory exhausted", "");
```

```
    strcpy (p->name, str);
    p->birth = p->death = zero_date;
    p->father = p->mother = (PERSON *) 0;

    /* ... and return the pointer */

    return p;
}
/**
 *  Determine sex.
 **/

sex_type
get_sex (char *str)
{
    /* Convert to upper case */

    strupcase (str, str);

    /* Should be either MALE or FEMALE */

    return (strcmp (str, "MALE") ? FEMALE : MALE);
}

/**
 *  Convert src to upper case in dest (toupper is a
 *  library function that converts [a-z] to [A-Z], and
 *  leaves all other characters untouched).
 **/

void
strupcase (char *dest, const char *src)
{
    while (*dest++ = toupper (*src++))
        ;
}
/**
 *  Convert str to a date. Terminate with a message
 *  on error.
 **/

DATE
get_date (char *str)
{
    char *ptr;              /* String pointer */
    register int i;     /* Month counter  */
    DATE date;          /* Converted date */

    /* '-' means unknown */

    if (!strcmp (str, "-"))
        date.month = date.day = date.year = 0;

    /* Convert str to DATE format */

    else {
        strupcase (str, str);
        for (i = 0; i < MONTHS; i++)
            if (!strncmp (str, month[i], strlen (month[i])))
                break;
        if (i >= MONTHS)
            ERROR("Invalid date ", str);
        date.month = i + 1;
```

```
        /* strtol is a library function that returns the
           long integer corresponding to the string in the
           first argument according to the number base in
           the third argument. Leading white space is
           ignored. If the second argument is not NULL,
           it will contain the address of the first
           non-digit character which terminates the
           conversion. */

        date.day = (short int)
            strtol (str + strlen (month[i]), &ptr, 10);
        date.year = (short int)
            strtol (ptr + 1, (char **) 0, 10);
    }
    return date;
}
/**
 *  Find out how many generations have to be printed. This
 *  function operates recursively by determining the
 *  number of generations above this one on both the
 *  mother's and father's side - the number of generations
 *  to be printed is the maximum of these numbers.
 **/

void
get_level (const PERSON *p)
{
    PERSON * dad, *mom;    /* Pointer to mother & father */

    /* Find father */

    for (dad = people; dad->name && dad != p->father; dad++)
        ;

    /* Find out how many generations above him */

    if (dad->name) {
        curr_level++;

        max_level = max(max_level, curr_level);
        get_level (dad);
        curr_level--
    }

    /* Find mother */

    for (mom = people; mom->name && mom != p->mother; mom++)
        ;

    /* Find out how many generations above her */

    if (mom->name) {
        curr_level++;
        max_level = max(max_level, curr_level);
        get_level (mom);
        curr_level--;
    }
}

/**
 *  C does not have an exponentiation operator - this
 *  function simulates it. Standard C has double
 *  pow(double x, double y) function. Since we want
 *  to perform only integer arithmetic, it is not
 *  necessary to involve complicated double precision
 *  operations.
 **/
```

```
power (int base, int exp)
{
    register int i, result;

    result = 1;
    for (i = 0; i < exp; i++)
        result *= base;
    return result;
}

/**
 *  Find the row position in the output image for
 *  this generation.
 **/

rowloc (int level, int offset)
{
    if (level == max_level)
        return (offset * 5 - 4);
    if (level == max_level - 1)
        return (offset * 10 - 6);
    return (rowloc (level + 1, offset * 2) +
            rowloc (level + 1, offset * 2 - 1)) / 2;
}

/**
 *  Generate the family tree in the output image by
 *  drawing this person, and then the family trees of
 *  their mother and father. The recursion stops when we
 *  run out of parents.
 **/

void
drawtree (const PERSON *p, int level, int offset)
{
    PERSON *mom, *dad;

    /* Draw this person */

    drawperson (p, rowloc (level, offset),
                                level * COLPLEV + 1);

    /* Draw father's family tree */

    for (dad = people; dad->name && dad != p->father; dad++)
        ;
    if (dad->name)
        drawtree (dad, level + 1, offset * 2 - 1);

    /* Draw mother's family tree */

    for (mom = people; mom->name && mom != p->mother; mom++)
        ;
    if (mom->name)
        drawtree (mom, level + 1, offset * 2);
}

/**
 *  Print date.
 **/

char *
put_date (const DATE *date)
{
    static char words[25];   /* Buffer for date in words */
    sprintf (words, "%s %d, %d", month[date->month - 1],
    date->day, date->year);
```

```
        return words;
}

/**
 * Draw a person in the output image, complete with
 * name and dates of birth and death.
**/

void
drawperson (const PERSON *p, int row, int col)
{
    char *d;                    /* Date buffer */

    /* Copy in name (memcpy is a library function which
       copies data from its second parameter to its first
       for a length in bytes of its third parameter) ...*/

    memcpy (pixel(row, col + 1), p->name, strlen (p->name));
    memcpy (pixel(row + 1, col), NAMELINE,
        sizeof(NAMELINE) - 1);

    /* ... and birth date, if it exists ... */

    if (p->birth.year) {
        memcpy (pixel(row + 2, col), " b.", 3);
        d = put_date (&(p->birth));
        memcpy (pixel(row + 2, col + 4), d, strlen (d));
    }

    /* ... and date of death */

    if (p->death.year) {
        memcpy (pixel(row + 3, col), " d.", 3);
        d = put_date (&(p->death));
        memcpy (pixel(row + 3, col + 4), d, strlen (d));
    }
}

/**
 * Print the output image.
**/

void
printtree (void)
{
    int i;

    for (i = 0; i < totrows; i++)
        printf ("%.*s\n", totcols, pixel(i + 1, 1));
}

/**
 * Put vertical lines into output image.
**/

void
vlines (void)
{
    register int i, j, k;

    for (i = 1; i <= max_level; i++)
        for (j = 1; j < power (2, i); j += 2)
            for (k = rowloc (i, j) + 1;
                 k <= rowloc (i, j + 1) + 1; k++)
                *(pixel(k, i * COLPLEV + 1)) = '|';
}

[ style 66.6 ]
```

*Example 9.4*

```
#ifndef FAMILY_H
#define FAMILY_H
/* ---------------------------------------------------
 * FAMILY.H - header file for FAMILY.C, family tree printer
 * -------------------------------------------------*/

/* To make the application portable, we will provide a set
   of macros. The macros behave in different ways
   depending on whether the compiler is standard ANSI C or
   not. All conformant implementations are required to
   define the __STDC__ constant. This constant can be used
   in making programs portable across ANSI and non-ANSI
   compilers.                                           */

#include <stdio.h>         /* provided on most C compilers */

#ifdef __STDC__
    /* ANSI standard C compiler */
    #include <stdlib.h>  /* defined by the standard */
    #include <string.h>  /* defined by the standard */
    #include <ctype.h>   /* defined by the standard */

    /* The following preprocessor macro will be used in
       function prototypes */
    #define PROT(x)     x
#else
    /* Older, non-standard compiler - it is necessary to
       define only those functions which do not return
       integer values */
    void exit ();
    char *strtok (), *malloc (), *strcpy (),
         *memset (), *memcpy ();
    long strtol ();

    /* The following preprocessor macro will be used in
       function prototypes.  Please note that '#'
       character must be in the first column for non-ANSI
       compilers. */
#define ASTR          *
#define PROT(x)     (/ASTR x ASTR/)

/* Define NULL if it isn't defined already */
#ifndef NULL
#define NULL         ((char *) 0)
#endif

#endif /* end of environment specific considerations */

typedef struct {
    short int month;    /* Month of year: 1 -> 12   */
    short int day;      /* Day of month: 1 -> 31    */
    short int year;     /* Year: 1 -> 1987          */
} DATE;

typedef enum {MALE, FEMALE} sex_type;

typedef struct person {
    char *name;               /* Name of person          */
    sex_type sex;             /* Sex                     */
    DATE birth;               /* Date of birth           */
    DATE death;               /* Date of death
                                 (0 year ==> still alive) */
    struct person *mother     /* Pointer to mother       */
    struct person *father;    /* Pointer to father       */
```

```
} PERSON;

/* Maximum length of an input line */
#define LINESIZE    128

/* Valid separators between fields in input line */
#define SEPSTRING   ":\n"

/* Width of one output column */
#define COLPLEV     18
/* Months in a year */
#define MONTHS      12

/* Maximum width of a name */
#define NAMELINE    "------------------"

/* Maximum value of x and y */
#define max(x,y)    ((x) > (y) ? (x) : (y))

/* Position in output array of row r column c */
#define pixel(r,c) (space + ((r) - 1) * totcols + (c) - 1)

/* Error handling macro */
#define ERROR(msg,data) \
  { fprintf (stderr,"%s%s\n",msg, data); exit (1); }

/* Function prototypes */
PERSON *get_name PROT((const char *name));
DATE get_date PROT((char *date_str));
sex_type get_sex PROT((char *sex_str));
void strupcase PROT((char *dest, const char *src));
void get_level PROT((const PERSON *person));
int power PROT((int base, int exp));
int rowloc PROT((int base, int exp));
void drawtree PROT((const PERSON *person, int level, int offset));
char *put_date PROT((const DATE *date));
void drawperson PROT((const PERSON *person, int row, int col));
void printtree PROT((void));
void vlines PROT((void));

#endif

/* ------------ family.h - ENDS --------------- */
```

## Input to the program might look like

```
* Input for ftree.c program

* Family tree of Michael Soren

Michael Soren:male:Aug 18,1958:-:Howard Soren:Toni Grossman

Toni Grossman:female:Sep 10,1932:-:Abraham Grossman:
                                        Erna Salzberg

Howard Soren:male:May 11,1930:-:Charles Sorkowitz:
                                        Minnie Sorkowitz

Abraham Grossman:male:Feb 24,1894:Apr 14,1966:
                                        Aria Grossman:Mindel Wurzel

Erna Salzberg:female:Sep 13,1896:Feb 12,1970:
                                        Jonah Salzberg:Chaya Weiser

Charles Sorkowitz:male:May 1,1895:Apr 14,1980:
                                        Harris Sorkowitz:Goldie Eglewitz

Minnie Sorkowitz:female:Dec 1,1898:Sep 24,1966:
                                        Nathan Sorkowitz:Etka Cohen
```

in which case the output for the pedigree chart of Michael Soren would look like

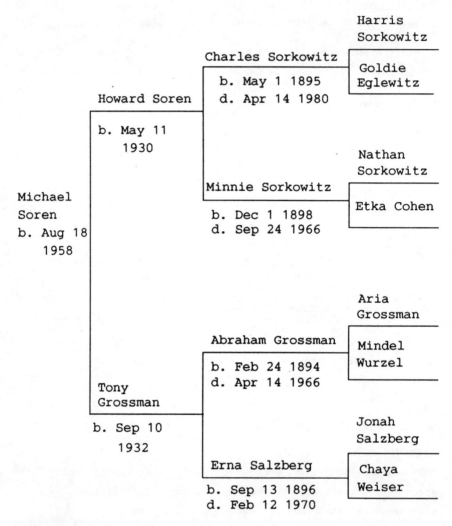

The program is commented well enough to be self-explanatory, but there are a number of features which are worthy of further explanation. Firstly, there are some standard functions used, such as *memset* and *strtok*, which are part of a run-time library defined by the ANSI standard. The library and the corresponding header files may or may not be present on your particular installation. The ones we have used are standard on the UNIX system, but may be different in other implementations. In any case, the functions are mostly straightforward to duplicate and, if missing, may be built by you in an effort to come closer to the standard C implementation.

Secondly, the mechanism for passing arguments into the program from the command line is demonstrated. In order that a program be as flexible as possible, it is important to parameterise it in the same way that you would parameterise any other function. In this case, the parameter is the name of the person whose pedigree chart is to be printed. The standard C specifies that implementations in "hosted" environments may specify arguments to the top level *main* function. "Hosted" means environments in which the applications are run under control of the host operating system. If provided, there must be two such arguments: the first one is an integer specifying the number of character strings passed to the pplication, and the second one is an array of character pointers containing addresses of the strings. All commonly found environments implement this ANSI C recommendation and pass to the application a set of character strings containing arguments supplied to the program on the command line starting its execution.

Thirdly, notice that the functions *get_level* and *drawtree* are recursive, which is a common feature of programs which manipulate data structures. Any one person's family tree consists of two sub-trees - the family trees of both their mother and their father. *drawtree* utilises this fact to draw the person's family tree by drawing first the person, and then the family trees of their mother and father; *get_level* determines the number of generations to be printed, which is simply one more than the maximum of the number of generations in either the mother's or father's tree.

And finally, note how provision is made for the input data to contain comment lines - this simple feature allows commentary to be included within data files to explain, for example, what the data are, or how they are to be used.

## SUMMARY

The theory and practice of data structures is a complicated topic, and one which is largely beyond the scope of this book. What we have presented is the basic tools - pointers, structures and dynamically allocated storage - which will allow you to generate arbitrarily complex data structures.

The thing to remember is that pointers are the equivalent in data structures of *goto*'s in control structures. It is as easy to finish up with unruly data structures as it is to generate "spaghetti code", and both are usually indicative of lack of forethought. The representation of data requires as much thought as the algorithm which manipulates it, and often the two are inextricably linked, in the sense that a poor design of either may cause the other to be unnecessarily complex and clumsy. The book *Algorithms + Data Structures = Programs* by Wirth (1976) is an excellent illustration of the way in which algorithms and data structures interact.

# 10 The C Preprocessor

We have already introduced the C preprocessor directives *#include* and *#define* for file inclusion and symbol definition capabilities. In this chapter, we expand the discussion to include all other capabilities of the preprocessor such as the *#undef* directive, the use of the conditional compilation directives *#if, #ifdef, #ifndef, #else, #elif* and *#endif*, string concatenation and token pasting. In addition, parameters for the *#define* directive are introduced to yield a more powerful macro facility. Some of these facilities have been defined recently in the ANSI standard and may not be available on your implementation.

Note that the C preprocessor is not part of the compiler; it is a macro processor which is used prior to compilation to perform textual substitutions and file inclusion. It has no knowledge of C syntax, and could equally well be used to process text in any language, including natural language. The results of the processed text are passed to the C compiler for subsequent translation.

## #define

In its simplest form, *#define* is used to associate a symbol with a value:

```
#define ENTRIES    100
```

If the value changes, we need only change it in the place where it is declared. A definition may refer to previously defined symbols, as in:

```
#define ARRAYSIZE    (ENTRIES+1)
```

The parentheses surrounding the substitution string are not mere formality; if *ARRAYSIZE* is used in the following context,

```
char array[ARRAYSIZE*4];
```

then omitting the parentheses would allocate an array of 104 bytes (100 + 1 * 4) instead of the intended 404 ((100 + 1) * 4).

During expansion of the symbol defined by the *#define* directive, the name of the symbol is not expanded again to avoid infinite loops.

For example

```
#define DONT_DO_IT_AGAIN    (DONT_DO_IT_AGAIN+1)
```

will not attempt to expand the second occurrence of *DONT_DO_IT_AGAIN* and will pass *(DONT_DO_IT_AGAIN+1)* to the compiler.

In Chapters 1 and 2, when we discussed the use of the *#define* directive to define constant text, we gave the example,

```
#define CLEAR    printf("\033Y")
```

to define the sequence necessary to clear the screen on a Lear Siegler ADM5.


## MACRO PARAMETERS

The *#define* directive is useful in its ability to substitute arbitrary text for a symbol. Here, we see how that capability can be expanded by providing arguments with a macro definition. As an example, consider a macro useful for debugging which prints out a trace message when a function is entered:

```
#define DB_ENTER    printf("Entering a function\n")
```

We could place this statement at the beginning of each function:

```
my_function ()
{
    DB_ENTER;
    .
    .
    .
```

This macro, in itself is not very useful, since it does not say which function is being entered, and the flow of logic may not be easy to understand. Fortunately, we can provide an argument (the function name) with the macro invocation if we define the macro as:

```
#define DB_ENTER(x)    printf("Entering %s\n", x)
```

Then, the statement at the beginning of each function could look like:

```
my_function ()
{
    DB_ENTER("my_function");
    .
    .
    .
```

After the DB_ENTER macro is substituted, the printf will arrange to print out "Entering my_function", which can be useful in examining the flow of control.

Similarly, we could define a macro to tell us when control is leaving a function, and the returning value. We could define:

```
#define DB_RETURN(x) {printf("Returning %d\n", x); return(x);}
```

so that if the above function were written as

```
my_function ()
{
    DB_ENTER("my_function");
    .
    .
    .
    DB_RETURN(69);
}
```

and the output would look like:

```
Entering my_function
Returning 69
```

This type of information can be very useful when trying to trace what's happening inside a program.

We could combine this with conditional compilation directives so that output would only be printed if a certain symbol, such as DEBUG were defined:

```
#ifdef DEBUG
#define DB_ENTER(x)  printf("Entering %s\n", x)
#define DB_RETURN(x) {printf("Returning %d\n", x); return(x);}
#else
#define DB_ENTER(x)
#define DB_RETURN(x) return(x)
#endif
```

The second definition of DB_ENTER specifies that the DB_ENTER(x) text should be substituted by nothing. Then, the program could be coded as before, but would only produce trace output if it was compiled with the symbol DEBUG defined. If the symbol DEBUG were not defined, no extra code would be generated into the program.

Macro parameters can also be used to simplify complex expressions or structure references. In the example 9.4 where a PERSON structure was declared, we could define a macro to easily access the name of a person's paternal grandfather:

```
#define GRANDPA(p)      (p->father->father.name)
```

Despite a lot of similarities between parameterised *#define* macros and regular function calls we have to realise that functions and macros are really quite different. Macros are expanded by the preprocessor and produce inline code without any function calls being made. There are two direct results of this behaviour. Firstly, there is no type checking of the macro arguments. This may result in subtle and difficult to trace problems if sufficient care is not taken. Secondly, preprocessor macros may produce side effects. Consider the following definitions

```
int
square (int a)
{
    return (a * a);
}
```

```
#define SQUARE(a)     (a) * (a)
```

and let us assume that *square* and *SQUARE* are called as in:

```
int in=5;
int out;

/* first call */
out = square(in++);

/* second version */
out = SQUARE(in++);
```

The effect of the call to *square(in++)* is *in=6* and *out=25* because only the value of *in* is passed to the function and *in* is subsequently incremented. The effect of executing *SQUARE(in++)* is *in=7* and *out=30*. This is easy to appreciate once the macro expansion is written out:

```
/* the second version expands to: */
out = (in++) * (in++);
/* in is incremented twice */
```

One must be very careful while using macros which can potentially be called with expressions as arguments. Conforming standard C implementations are allowed to provide macro versions of functions, provided that the macros are "safe", that is, evaluate their arguments only once, and provided that un-defining the macro will result in using a true library function. This last condition is very useful during the debugging phase. It may be useful to generate true function calls in order to use some debugging facilities which can stop program execution upon entry into a function. Such function calls can later be replaced by preprocessor macros to speed up program execution, since macros are expanded in place to a string of C statements and do not suffer from the overhead of function calls.

## #undef

To make the preprocessor forget its definition of *SQUARE*, we can write:

```
#undef SQUARE
```

and thereafter the preprocessor will leave all occurrences of SQUARE alone, passing it unsubstituted to the compiler. Should we have both a macro and a true function versions of *SQUARE*, undefining it would make sure that the function is used. Undefining of a symbol not previously defined is allowed and is simply ignored by the preprocessor.

## CONDITIONAL COMPILATION

When we write programs, it is advantageous to try to write them in such a way so they are portable; that is, they can be moved to another machine of differing architecture or operating system without changing the source code. They should perform the same function on the new machine as they did on the old one, even though the underlying code and implementation may be different. This increases programmer efficiency so that it is no longer necessary to re-code existing functions for a new machine. The preprocessor makes this task easier with the availability of conditional compilation.

Consider the example of clearing a terminal screen. If all terminals in the world were Lear Siegler ADM5's, the definition of *CLEAR* would be the same in all cases. However, because different terminals use different sequences to accomplish the same function, this definition must be modified. On a DEC VT100, the statement would have to be:

```
#define CLEAR    printf("\033[2J")
```

The conditional compilation statements allow us to include certain sections of code based upon specified conditions. Thus, we can combine the two *CLEAR* definitions so that the desired one is defined for either situation. We can write:

```
#ifdef VT100
#define CLEAR    printf("\033[2J")
#else
#define CLEAR    printf("\033Y")
#endif
```

The above construction says that if the symbol *VT100* is defined to the preprocessor, use the first definition of *CLEAR*; otherwise, use the second. Conditional compilation proceeds until the *#endif* directive is encountered. Now, all that is needed in order to use this program for a VT100 is to include a line at the top of the program which defines the symbol *VT100*:

```
#define VT100
```

If we wanted to, we could define the sequence for all other available terminals so that the same source code would run unchanged. Please note that it is sufficient to just *#define* the symbol without actually assigning any particular value to it.

We can make similar constructions to define symbols only if they are not already defined, as in the following:

```
#ifndef NULL
#define NULL     ((char *) 0)
#endif
```

This construction defines the symbol *NULL* only if it was not previously defined.

We can make the condition for compilation more complex by using the *#if* directive. With the *#if* directive, the condition must be a non-zero constant at compile time in order for the lines through *#endif* to be passed to the compiler. Making programs machine independent then becomes a matter of defining a symbol and testing for it to indicate the target processor. Then, definitions are made on the basis of which type machine the program is compiled for:

```
/* assuming that the code contains one or more
   directives of the form: */
#define mc68k     1

/* we can write: */

#if mc68k || i286 || i386
    .
    /* Set definitions for the Motorola 68000 based
       or Intel 80286 or 80386 processor */
    .
#endif
#if u3b2 || u3b5 || u3b15 || u3b20
    .
    /* Set definitions for the AT&T 3b processors */
    .
#endif
#if uts || u370
    .
    /* Set definitions for the Amdahl
       and IBM processors */
    .
#endif
```

Please note that in order for symbols to be used in checks such as above, a particular value should be assigned to the symbol defined. Logical operators recognised by the C preprocessor behave in the same way as the corresponding language operators. Non-zero values are assumed to be true, while zero is assumed to be false. Just defining a symbol without providing a value for it is equivalent to defining it with the value of 0 for the purpose of evaluation in logical expressions. Also please note that the preprocessor does not report errors if a symbol is not defined. The symbol is simply assumed to have a value of 0 in logical expressions.

Directive *#elif* is equivalent to the directive *#else* followed by *#if* and can be used as shorthand in specifying multiple nested conditions.

Very similar to *#ifdef* and *#ifndef* directives but much more flexible is the *defined* operator. Using this operator, several checks may be combined in a single *#if* directive as in

```
#if defined(BLACK_GUARDIAN) && !defined(WHITE_GUARDIAN)
#define IN_TROUBLE     1
#endif
```

The *defined* operator has been introduced by the C standard and may not be available on your system.

Although the examples presented above show only preprocessor directives

(*#define, #undef*) used within the conditional compilation directives, C source code can be placed there as well to perform different functions under different circumstances. Some examples of this may be found in the section on preprocessor techniques later in this chapter.

## TOKEN PASTING AND STRING CONVERSIONS

Any two strings separated only by white space, that is blanks, tabs, newline or page eject characters, are concatenated by a conformant preprocessor. This may be useful in cases of long character strings such as in

```
printf ("The first part of a very long "
                "character string\n");
```

which becomes

```
printf ("The first part of a very long character string\n");
```

before being passed to the compiler. This behaviour may be useful in some cases; it is however essential for correct behaviour of a new # operator.

The C standard introduced two new preprocessor operators dealing directly with tokens in the replacement list of a macro. The # operator converts its argument to a string as in the following example:

```
#define PRT_VALUE(X) printf ("The value of " #X " is:%d\n", X)
int answer = 42;
```

We may want to print the value in order to trace the execution of our program as follows:

```
PRT_VALUE(answer);
```

The above fragment of code is transformed by the preprocessor into:

```
printf ("The value of " "answer" " is %d\n", answer);
```

which in turn becomes:

```
printf ("The value of answer is %d\n", answer);
```

given that the adjacent strings are concatenated.

A somewhat complementary capability dealing with non-string arguments is provided by a new token pasting operator. The new operator denoted by *##* takes the left and right operands and concatenates them before passing the resulting string to the compiler. For example:

```
#define MAKE_VAR(a, b)      (a##b)
```

when called as in

```
int MAKE_VAR(value, _one);
```

becomes

```
int value_one;
```

## ADDITIONAL DIRECTIVES

Three additional directives are defined in the C standard and may not be available in your C implementation.

The preprocessor counts the source lines as it proceeds through the code. *#line* followed by a token or a macro resolving itself to a decimal number and an optional character string, can be inserted anywhere in the source code, and indicates that the following line has the given number and came from the file indicated. This facility is used mainly by utilities which themselves produce a C code output, such as third party preprocessors, to maintain linkage between the line numbers of the original source and the produced C source. The *#line* directive directly sets the values of __LINE__ and __FILE__ symbols described in the next section.

The *#error* directive followed by any set of macros or other preprocessing tokens causes a diagnostic message containing these tokens to be displayed at compile time. This directive is typically used in conjunction with *#if* directives to diagnose some undesirable compile time conditions. For example:

```
#if !defined(WHITE_GUARDIAN) && !defined(BLACK_GUARDIAN)
#error "At least one of the two guardians must be present"
#endif
```

The *#pragma* directive allows for implementation specific behaviour. The standard specifies only that any *#pragma* not recognised by the particular implementation should be ignored. This allows for some limited expansion of the preprocessor capabilities in an implementation defined manner. For example, an implementation may allow different compiler behaviour based on various switches, or arguments passed to the compiler. Some or all of these switches may have their *#pragma* equivalents, thus allowing the programs to influence the way in which they are compiled. It should be stressed that any such behaviour is implementation specific and depending on it for correct compilation or execution of programs may lead to unpleasant surprises if wide portability is intended.

## PREDEFINED MACRO NAMES

Several predefined macro names have been specified by the standard. Some if not all of them are probably defined in your implementation. The names are defined by the preprocessor itself and can be used throughout the code as if specified by *#define* statements.

__LINE__ contains the line number of the source statement currently processed by the preprocessor. The value is reset to 1 at the begining of each source file.

__FILE__ contains the name of the file currently processed by the preprocessor.

__DATE__ contains the date when preprocessing began and remains constant throughout the execution of the preprocessor.

__TIME__ contains the time when preprocessing began and remains constant throughout the execution of the preprocessor.

__STDC__ is defined to be 1 by all conformant implementations and can be used in writing portable code.

The use of these constants and examples of other useful preprocessor applications are illustrated in the next section.


## PREPROCESSOR TECHNIQUES

We will now attempt to illustrate some of the preprocessor features described in the previous sections to produce a few useful tricks and techniques which can be used to advantage in everyday software development. The ideas presented in this section aspire to being helpful in producing more reliable and portable code.

In large, complicated programs, it is very common to have many header files which depend for some of their content on other header files. It is therefore unavoidable that many header files include many other header files, and that the program source files comprising the software product include various subsets of the header files. This situation often leads to multiple copies of the same header file being included in the same source module. While not always disastrous, multiple inclusions of the same header file in one source module lead to a longer compilation time and wasted machine resources. A very common way of avoiding such a situation is to define a constant uniquely identifying a header file and enclose the content of the entire file in an *#ifndef* directive like in the following:

```
/* let's assume this header file to be named local.h */
#ifndef __LOCAL_H /* if __LOCAL_H constant not defined - */
#define __LOCAL_H /* define it and */
              .     /* enter here all the statements */
              .     /* comprising the header file */
              .
#endif              /* end with #endif corresponding to the */
                    /* top level #ifndef */
```

Remembering that all *#define* constants are global throughout all header files comprising a software module, it is easy to see that the first copy of *local.h* will be processed and, among other things, will define __LOCAL_H. On subsequent inclusions of the same header file the constant is already defined and the content of the file is not processed again due to the *#ifndef* directive.

All but the smallest software projects require some control over which versions of what files are included in the particular version of the product.

Many sophisticated version control systems have been devised for that purpose. We may decide that for our small projects it is sufficient to just have a date and time stamp embedded in every module. This can be accomplished by defining a macro containing the stamp

```
#define ID_STRING   __FILE__  " as of " __DATE__ " at " __TIME__
```

and then including the following line in every module which we want to stamp

```
static char FileID[]=ID_STRING;
```

*FileID* of every file containing the above declaration will be embedded into the executable file. A simple tool may be written to scan the content of the executable file and search for all time stamps thus revealing which versions have been used to build it.

Given that function prototyping provides us with a benefit of automatic type checking and thus eliminates the errors stemming from argument and parameter mismatch, we should attempt to use this feature whenever possible. The trouble is that many compilers still do not support the full ANSI standard. In preparation for a wider availability of the standard compilers we should attempt to write programs which could be easily modified to take advantage of function prototyping once it becomes available on our installation. To that end, it may be prudent to incorporate the following set of macros as a standard for building function prototypes.

```
#ifdef __STDC__
    /* the following preprocessor macro will be used
       in function prototypes */
    #define PROT(x)    x
#else
    /* The following preprocessor macro will be used in
       function prototypes.  Please note that the '#'
       character must be in the first column for some
       non-ANSI compilers. */
    #define ASTR         *
    #define PROT(x)     (/ASTR x ASTR/)
#endif /* end of environment specific considerations */
```

For the conforming compilers, as indicated by the predefined macro *__STDC__*, we define macro *PROT* to just resolve to its argument. For non-conformant compilers, the macro will resolve to its argument enclosed in parenthesis and comment delimiters. *PROT* macro allows us to provide function prototypes of the following form

```
char *function PROT((int arg1, char *arg2));
```

and have it resolved to

```
char *function (/*(int arg1, char *arg2)*/);
```

and

```
char *function (int arg1, char *arg2);
```

for non-standard and standard compilers respectively. To be as widely portable as possible, we have defined an intermediate macro *ASTR*. In some older installations the symbol /**/ is used as a concatenation operator, equivalent to ## in ANSI C. You may want to experiment with the above on your system and directly substitute * for the *ASTR* macro. Also please note that the double parentheses while passing arguments to *PROT* are needed. The outer set is required to signal that *PROT* is a macro, and the inner set encloses a single argument, consisting in this case of a rather lengthy character string containing, among other things, commas.

It is often necessary to trace execution of a program during its development so that errors in algorithms or their implementations can be easily spotted. *TRACE* macros can be created for that purpose. Two separate macros for decimal and string values are needed. Alternatively one macro taking as arguments the variable name and its type can be provided.

```
#include <stdio.h>

#define TRACED(v) fprintf(stderr, "Value of " #v " in file " \
                  __FILE__ " at line %d is: %d\n", __LINE__, v)
#define TRACES(v) fprintf(stderr, "Value of " #v " in file " \
                  __FILE__ " at line %d is: %s\n", __LINE__, v)
```

The preprocessor in combination with *typedef* class allows for definition of application specific data types which may be tuned to the maximum allowable value for the type. For example, let us assume that the application processes types of sails and rigs found on contemporary sailing boats. The number of various sail types is not originally known, but is to be established later, after the software is written. We may decide in this situation to define a separate data type for the sail types as follows:

```
#if MAX_SAIL_TYPES <= 256
typedef SailType unsigned char;
#else
typedef SailType unsigned int;
#endif

SailType WinningSail;
```

Depending on the maximum allowable number of sail types, assuming that each sail type is represented by a unique number, the storage for the sail types is defined to be either *unsigned char* or *unsigned int*.

It is often useful to operate on variables declared as a generic address or pointer type. Standard C defines *void\** as a pointer to any data type, but it may not be available on many older implementations. To avoid this problem, a generic address type may be defined as follows:

```
#ifdef    STDC                       /* if standard C */
typedef caddr_t   void*;
#else
typedef caddr_t   char*;
#endif

caddr_t pointer_to_anything;
```

*pointer_to_anything* is defined in a portable fashion. On standard implementations, the new *void\** will be used. On compilers which do not support it, *char\** will be used instead. In both cases our intention to use *caddr_t* variables as generic pointers is clearly visible.

## SUMMARY

There are many reasons for utilising the C preprocessor's capabilities to perform text substitution within a program. Among them are:

- *#define*'d constants and macros can bedeclared in one place and used throughout the code; subsequent changes can be made once at the declaration, without having to search for every instance.

- Complexity can be hidden from the programmer without sacrificing efficiency or functionality so that program logic is not obscured by detail.

- Conditional compilation can be used to eliminate machine and other dependencies.

- Using names for constants improves the intelligibility of the code.

- Useful macros improving portability of the code can be defined.

# 11   Programming Style

Programming in any language is a skill acquired largely by experience and by observing the example of others. The way in which your programs are presented is a matter for personal taste. It is often a tradeoff between brevity and intelligibility. Although programming 'style' is often considered to be unquantifiable and assessable only in subjective terms, we have made an attempt, in an appendix, to identify those features of program layout and organisation that tend to make it more visually appealing and more easily comprehensible.

It is now realised that the lifetime of a program, and the cost of program maintenance, frequently done by someone other than the author, make considerations of clarity of expression often of equal importance with those of efficiency. This is especially true in the recent times when the cost of computing machines has been steadily declining and the costs associated with writing and maintaining the software have significantly increased. It is to the usually conflicting aims of clarity, conciseness and efficiency that we address our attention in this chapter.

## CLARITY

The clarity of a program is influenced by two principal factors: the way in which the program is presented visually, and the way in which the programming language constructs are used. The 'style score' that we have associated with all the programming examples throughout the book is a measure of the former. Appendix 1 gives a program to perform a style analysis on a C program according to certain criteria which we believe contribute directly to a program's readability. You may not agree entirely with the criteria that we have chosen, or with the importance that we attach to each criterion, but you will almost certainly agree that the second of the two versions of the program *detab* (which replaces all the tab characters in a file by the appropriate number of spaces), presented in example 11.1, is very much more intelligible than the first.

*Example 11.1*

```
#include  <stdio.h>

int
main (void)
{
    int c,i,tabs[132],col=1;
    settabs(tabs);
    while ((c=getchar())!=EOF)
        if (c=='\t')
            do {putchar(' ');col++;
                } while (!tabpos(col,tabs));
        else if (c=='\n') {putchar('\n'); col=1;}
            else {putchar(c); col++;}
}
settabs(int tabs[132])
{
    int i;
    for (i=1;i<=132;i++)
        if ((i%8)==1) tabs[i]=1;else tabs[i]=0;
}
tabpos(int col,int tabs[132])
{
    if (col>132) return(1);else return(tabs[col]);
}
```

[ style 39.1 ]

```
/***************************************************/
/* Detab - convert tabs to appropriate number of  */
/* spaces (transcribed from Kernighan & Plauger's */
/* "Software Tools")                               */
/***************************************************/

#include  <stdio.h>
#define   MAXLINE 132
#define   TAB_POS 8

main (void)
{
    int     c, i, tabs[MAXLINE], col=1;

    set_tabs (tabs);

    while ((c = getchar()) != EOF)
        /* Put spaces instead of tabs */
        if (c == '\t')
            do  { putchar ( ' ' ); col++; }
            while (!tab_pos (col, tabs));

        /* Newlines reset column counter */
        else if (c == '\n')
            { putchar ('\n'); col = 1; }

        /* Anything else is unchanged */
        else
            { putchar (c); col++; }
}
```

```
/* Set up tab positions every TAB_POS characters */

set_tabs (int tabs[MAXLINE])
{
    int     i;

    for (i = 1; i <= MAXLINE; i++)
        tabs[i] = ((i % TAB_POS) == 1 ? 1 : 0);
}

/* See if we're at a tab position */

tab_pos (int col, int tabs[MAXLINE])
{
    return ((col > MAXLINE) ? 1 : tabs[col]);
}

[ style 80.2 ]
```

The programs are equivalent, in the sense that they contain identical executable statements differently laid out. The 'bad' program could, of course, be very much worse, but then it would not be so typical of the kind of program that it is very tempting to write in a language that encourages brevity. In the authors' experience, programs written like this, with the intention of subsequent cosmetic improvement, tend to remain in their original format - there is little incentive to modify (even superficially) a working program. Automatic aids to 'beautifying' a program by introducing indentation, blank lines, etc. to reflect the program's structure are no substitute for a program thoughtfully written.

The criteria that we have chosen to use in the style analysis of our own programs are shown, in decreasing order of importance, in table 11.1.

Table 11.1

| Criterion | Weighting | Ideal range | |
|---|---|---|---|
| Module length | 15% | 10-25 | non-blank lines |
| Identifier length | 14% | 5-10 | characters |
| % comment lines | 12% | 15-25% | |
| % indentation | 12% | 24-48% | |
| % blank lines | 11% | 15-30% | |
| Characters per line | 9% | 12-25 | non-blank characters |
| Spaces per line | 8% | 4-10 | spaces |
| % #defines | 8% | 15-25% | of all identifiers |
| Reserved word usage | 6% | 16-30 | of available words |
| Include files | 5% | 3 | included files |

The relative weights and ideal ranges are not arbitrarily chosen, but rather are the result of careful tuning after analysis of programs that we recognised intuitively as 'good' or 'bad'. They may need modification to cater for individual preferences, or to reflect a particular 'house style'. Up to this point, all examples for which a style score is given are relatively small in size. Style scores for a number of large programs from the UNIX system are given in Berry and Meekings (1985).

The style analysis program does not pretend to measure, in anything more than the most rudimentary sense, the second factor contributing to clarity: the use of the language itself. As in so many things, in programming there is no 'right' answer - just a number of alternative ways of achieving the same ends. Invariably, some of those ways will be clumsy or obscure. This will most often be the result of either inexperience or poor design - experience of using a language brings with it a number of benefits: for example, being able to 'think in the language' avoids the clumsy type of construct that arises from the direct transliteration of an algorithm derived by a programmer more familiar with another language, and also being able to use effectively the programming 'tricks' that exist within any language (for example, in C, using

```
while (*str1++ = *str2++);
```

to copy a string); and poor initial design, failure to derive a complete solution before coding, is bound to yield a program that is a functional mess, badly structured and with poor lines of communication.


## CONCISENESS

There is a point, not always easy to identify, at which 'concise' becomes 'obscure'. Compare, for example, the random number generator program of example 6.2 with the functionally equivalent program of example 11.2. The gain in execution speed would have to be considerable to justify the inclusion of such a complex (but perfectly legal) statement in any program.

*Example 11.2*

```
#define maxint 32767
#define pshift 4
#define qshift 11

random(int range)
{
    static int n=1;

    return((n=((n=n^n>>pshift)^n<<qshift)&maxint)%(range+1));
}

[ style 45.2 ]
```

As a further example of a program that is concise to the point of obscurity, study the program of example 11.3, and try to determine its effect.

*Example 11.3*

```
#define LO 2
#define HI 1000

int
main(void)
{
    int i,j;

    for (i=LO; i<=HI; i++) {
        j=sum(i);
        if (j==i) printf("%d\n",i);
        else if (sum(j)==i) printf("%d %d\n",i,j);
    }
}

int
sum(int n)
{
    int s, f;

    s=1;
    for (f=2; f<n; f++)
        if (n%f==0) s+=f;
    return(s);
}
```

[ style 51.4 ]

Even with explanation, the program is very much more difficult to understand than is the equivalent program of example 11.4 which differs only by using more meaningful identifier names and having a helpful user interface. The program is in fact a generalisation of the perfect number program of example 5.6. Perfect numbers are a special case of 'amicable' numbers, which are pairs of numbers, each of whose sum of factors yields the other number; so that, for example, the sum of the factors of 220 is 284, while the sum of the factors of 284 is 220: 220 and 284 are amicable numbers.

*Example 11.4*

```
#define LO 2
#define HI 1000

int
main (void)
{
    int number, sum;

    for (number = LO; number <= HI; number++) {
        sum = factorsum (number);
        if (sum == number)
            printf ("%d is perfect\n", number);
```

```
        else if (factorsum (sum) == number)
            printf ("%d,%d are amicable\n", number, sum);
    }
}

int
factorsum (int num)
{
    int fsum, factor;

    fsum = 1;
    for (factor = 2; factor < num; factor++)
        if (num % factor == 0)
            fsum += factor;
    return (fsum);
}
```

[ style 66.5 ]

C is undoubtedly a concise language, and encourages the terse representation of complex ideas. Such power should be judiciously used.

## EFFICIENCY

The price that is paid for writing programs in any high-level language is in program size and execution time. Unless either of these is particularly critical, the advantages, in terms of productivity and maintenance costs, far outweigh the disadvantages.

C has a number of features that are more usually found in a lower-level language, to the extent that the correspondence between a C program and the machine code to which it compiles is often very close. The effect of this is to reduce the overheads resulting from the translation process very much more than for other contemporary languages. Some C compilers will offer the user an optional optimisation phase, but an alert and informed user is usually the best optimiser of a program. C provides some help in this: for example, the type specifiers *int* or *char* may be preceded by the storage class specifier *register* thus:

```
register int   n;

register char *sptr;
```

This is interpreted by the compiler as an indication that these identifiers will be heavily used and should, if possible, have storage space in registers. If the compiler is able to do this, then shorter, faster programs should result.

Nevertheless, the program has not yet been written that could not be written better or executed faster. A software tool, *prof*, available on the UNIX operating system, can be used to produce an 'execution profile' of a program, in terms of, for each function, the number of times that it was called, and the percentage of total execution time that it accounted for. This is of obvious benefit, since there is relatively little return from devoting time to improving the efficiency either of functions that are infrequently called, or of those that occupy only a small percentage of the execution time. Thus, we can concentrate on those areas where our efficiency tuning efforts would be most rewarded.

As an illustration of the kind of improvements that can be made, the following results were obtained by profiling an early version of RatC (mentioned in the Introduction), a program that compiles a subset of the C programming language:

| Function | Number of calls | % of execution time |
|----------|-----------------|---------------------|
| alpha    | 382,521         | 10.1                |
| findmac  | 3,594           | 10.0                |
| asreq    | 334,421         | 8.6                 |
| numeric  | 381,794         | 6.4                 |
| an       | 379,550         | 5.6                 |

In other words, the three functions *alpha, numeric,* and *an* (which simply check a character parameter to see whether it is alphabetic, numeric, and alphanumeric, respectively) accounted for a quarter of the execution time, and *findmac* (which is essentially a table look-up to determine whether a symbol has been previously defined as a macro) also made significant contribution. When it is known that RatC was compiling a program that consisted of only about 50,000 characters, the number of calls of *alpha, numeric* and *an* should cause concern.

*Example 11.5*

```
/* test if a given character is alphabetic */
alpha (char c)
{
    c = c & 127;    /* strip off the high order bit */
    return (((c >= 'a') & (c <= 'z'))
            ((c >= 'A') & (c <= 'Z'))
             (c == '_'));
}

/* test if a given character is numeric */
numeric (char c)
{
    c = c & 127;
    return ((c >= '0') & (c <= '9'));
}
/* test if a given character is alphanumeric */
an (char c)
{
    return ((alpha (c)) | (numeric (c)));
}
```

[ style 40.7 ]

The character checking functions were originally defined as shown in example 11.5. Two significant changes were made: firstly, the high order bit was stripped off once and for all on input, to avoid unnecessary repetition; and secondly, the function *an* was made to check explicitly for the requisite characters, avoiding the overheads incurred by the two function calls. In the latest version of RatC, these three functions account for less than 5 per cent of the execution time. As is typically the case in most programs, time can be traded for space and vice versa. The three functions could be implemented by table lookups, the way C library character classification functions described in Chapter 12 are normally implemented. Correct choice of various tradeoffs is a part of the design process of any software system, as indeed it is a part of any engineering activity.

The way in which the macro definitions were stored was changed from a simple table of the form

| name | definition | name | definition | name | definition | ... |
|------|-----------|------|-----------|------|-----------|-----|

to a more complex one of the form

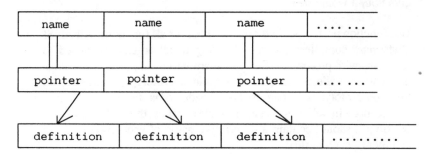

in order to speed up the time taken to perform a linear search for a particular name. This is very important in view of the fact that the majority of searches will be unsuccessful, requiring a search through the entire table. The execution time for this function was thus reduced to a quarter of its original value, at the expense of a little extra memory. Although the function could still be improved, perhaps by introducing a more complicated searching algorithm, we believe the simplicity/efficiency trade-off to be about right.

Improving the efficiency of a program is not always an easy, or even desirable task. For a small program, the effects may not be noticeable; for a large program, run infrequently, the time invested may not be worth while. For a heavily utilised program, such as a compiler, however, attention to the time-critical, bottleneck areas can give a significant improvement in performance.

## DEFENSIVE PROGRAMMING

Throughout the book we have attempted to emphasise the importance of the interface between the program and its environment. Any program should take every possible precaution to ensure that it does not fail, and that, if it does, the failure is 'graceful', which is to say that it should provide the naive user with sufficient information to correct, or work around, the problem.

This section is concerned with 'bulletproofing' a program, and consists for the most part of a series of suggestions which you should bear in mind whenever writing programs - they are often the result of painfully acquired experience! If you follow our advice, you are certain to avoid at least some of the common pitfalls of porting programs from one machine to another, which, contrary to popular opinion, is not nearly as simple as it is supposed to be.

(a)   Use lint. 'Lint' is a UNIX system utility which is commonly available on a variety of other systems. It performs a much more rigorous check than does the compiler on such things as type consistency, use of uninitialised variables, and correspondence between function arguments and parameters. If we had only one piece of advice to give you, it would be this.

(b)   Use function prototypes and provide them for all functions. All ANSI C standard compilers do type checking of all arguments passed to functions with prototypes. Some of them will even produce warnings if a call is made to a function without a prototype. Gathering all function prototypes in one or more header files and then including the headers in all appropriate modules makes the task easy. The prototypes should contain a descriptive name of each argument and comments, such as this:

```
/* returns a degree to which the universe is real
   measured in DIBs (disbelief and bewilderment) */
int test_reality (char *question, /* question to be asked */
                  char **answers, /* array of reasonable
                                              answers */
                  enum GODS entity); /* whom to ask or 0 if
                                       cannot make up mind */
```

(c)   Check input data. At the end of chapter 3, we mentioned that input data is nearly always beyond the control of the programmer. You should check the integrity of all data which are derived from outside the program to make sure that they are within prescribed values. If you don't know what the prescribed values are, at least check that the value won't cause a runtime error - zero values used for division are an obvious example.

(d)   Check function arguments. By a similar reasoning to the previous point, if you assume that function arguments are always sane, you'll be caught unawares when, at some time in the future, you 'steal' the code to put in some other program where you haven't been quite so careful.

(e)   Check return values from functions. If a function (either yours or a system-provided one) returns a value, check it before continuing. Nearly all system-provided functions return values, and it's good practice to make yours do so too. Never assume that a function will always be successful - it always will be, except when you don't check it!

(f)   Don't rely on uninitialised variables. Variables of storage class *static* can be safely assumed to start with zero value; variables of storage class *automatic* start with garbage values. While this may be true, if you don't explicitly initialise them, the time will come when you change the storage class of one of your variables without changing the program logic, and wonder why it doesn't work anymore.

(g)   Don't exploit implementation dependent features. On some systems, a pointer occupies the same storage space as an integer. If you use that fact, your program probably won't work on another, dissimilar, machine. A slightly more insidious example arises from something we said at the end of chapter 6 - 'no ordering is implied among operators with the same priority'. Parentheses in an expression control precedence and associativity, but not order of evaluation, which is to say that the expression $a + b + c$ could be evaluated by adding $a$ to $b$, and adding the result to $c$, or by adding $b$ to $c$, and the result to $a$. Normally this causes no problem, but consider the expression

```
y = x++ + x;
```

If $x$ initially has the value 1, what value does $y$ have after the assignment? 2? 4? The answer is that it's impossible to say - of course, on any particular implementation, it will always be evaluated the same way, but this is not true of the same program running on a different machine. The assignment should have been written as

```
x++; y = x + x;
```

or

```
y = x + x; x++;
```

depending on what you intend.

(h)　Don't use side effects in macro calls. The seemingly innocuous macro

```
#define MAX(a,b)   (a < b ? b : a)
```

when invoked by

```
z = MAX (x++, y);
```

leaves *x* with a different result depending on whether it is greater or less than *y*, because the preprocessor only performs textual substitution so that, in practice, the macro expands to

```
z = (x++ < y ? y : x++);
```

(i)　Use parentheses in expressions. If you are unsure of operator precedence, or if the expression that you are formulating is complex don't be afraid to use parentheses to make it clearer. It adds nothing to the execution time, but a great deal to the comprehensibility.

(j)　Don't corrupt C with the preprocessor. It's very easy, using the preprocessor, to make C look like some other language. If you are fond of Pascal, you might be tempted to write

```
#define BEGIN    {
#define END      }
       .
       .
       .
```

but the result will be a confusion of neither one language, nor the other.

(k)　Use the right type of variable. Don't use an *int* when a *char* will do - for example with a truth value; or an *int* where you mean a pointer. You not only save space, you give a program like 'lint' a much better chance of detecting potential problems.

(l)　Exit gracefully. A program should never fail inexplicably - provide the user with sufficient information as to the cause of the failure that he understands what has gone wrong and what he can do to correct it. Catch and process signals and provide enough additional information for the user to correct the cause for abnormal termination.

(m)　Don't rely on defaults. Often a system provided function will offer default values for some of its arguments. If you take advantage of that you run the risk of your program no longer working should those defaults ever change.

(n)   Be very careful and thoughtful while using dynamic memory management. Bad pointers, referring to an area of memory not allocated for use by the program and freeing too early or not freeing at all the storage space which is allocated to the process, are probably the most common problems in a C program. Each variable in a C program has a scope, that is a period of time and an area of code in which the variable is accessible and contains valid data. For example, *automatic* variables are accessible from within functions which defined them and cease to exist when the function returns. In the case of dynamic memory allocated via calls to *malloc*, it is up to the programmer to free the memory allocated and be sure that referencing it is allowed at any given time. By analogy, it is very helpful to think about scoping the dynamic storage during program design and always make sure that the dynamically allocated variables remain in the scope of the program for as long as they are needed and no longer.

(o)   Do it right the first time. It is the authors' experience that there is never time to go back to an already written piece of software and improve its behaviour in some odd cases or restructure it for the sake of readability or ease of maintenance.

If you are familiar with other programming languages such as Pascal or PL/1, there are several additional pitfalls of which you should be aware.

(p)   Beware of the difference between = and ==. If you are used to a language which uses the same operator for assignment and equivalence, sometime you will fall into the trap. It sounds easy to remember, but we have all forgotten it at some time!   Some compilers produce warning messages if a conditional statement contains an assignment as a top level operator.

(q)   You will recall that C passes all its function arguments by value. In order to make the argument modifiable by a function, its address must be passed. Passing a value and not an address of an argument to a function, especially functions such as *scanf*, is another one of the very common mistakes.

(r)   Many Pascal programmers have a difficult time remembering the difference between character arrays and character pointers. With declarations like this:

```
char *str_ptr, str[81];
```

it is possible to assign an address of a constant string to *str_ptr* like in:

```
str_ptr = "Hello galaxy";
```

We have to remember that *str_ptr* is not capable of holding the entire string, but is just a pointer which is assigned an address of the string. In the case of *str*, however, we cannot say

```
str = "Hello galaxy";   /* WRONG */
```

*str* and the literal string occupy two different areas of storage. *str* is a character array and we have to copy each character of the "Hello galaxy" string into the array thus:

```
strcpy (str, "Hello galaxy");
```

(s)   Many languages use a comma to delimit indices in multidimensional arrays, such as *a = b[i,j];*. This statement will compile in C but is probably not what you intended.

(t)   Each *case* statement in C is executed in turn until a *break* statement is encountered. This is different in many other languages in which only one *case* statement is executed at any given time.

## SUMMARY

Programming style and program efficiency are contentious issues: some will maintain that 'style' is so personal that it is impossible to lay down more than vague guidelines, others that it is the business of compilers and optimisers to worry about efficiency. What should never be forgotten is that, as we said in the introduction, programming is communication, and the communication operates at different levels: between the program and the computer, between the program and the user, and between the program and its maintainer.

It is all too tempting in a language like C to sacrifice clarity for conciseness and efficiency. There are relatively few occasions on which careful consideration of the method by which a program achieves its results (as in the macro table organisation, above) would not yield the desired effect, without the need to resort to tricky obscure code.

The power of C, used properly, can be exploited to produce programs that are elegant, concise and, above all, intelligible.

# 12 The Standard C Libraries

The definition of standard C specifies a library which must be present in any conforming implementation. The functions supplied in the library are declared in several header files, divided according to the type of services provided by the functions. Many of the functions defined by the standard are supplied even in older implementations and most of them are probably present on your system, even though the original C definition did not specify any of them. The header files declaring the library functions also specify macros and variables which may be used by the applications to accomplish various tasks as described below. Additionally, the headers may define macros with the same names as the corresponding library functions, provided that the macros can safely be used in any place and with any set of arguments with which the corresponding function can be called. In particular, it must be guaranteed that macro arguments are evaluated only once. The applications can always ensure that a true library function rather than a macro is called by using the *#undef* preprocessor directive. It can also be done locally by enclosing the function name in parentheses. For syntactic reasons, the closing parenthesis will prevent the interpretation of the identifier as a macro.

Since not all of the header files and corresponding library functions may be defined on your system, it may be useful to compare the list of standard functions, macros and type definitions to what is available on your system. Anticipating the arrival of a standard compiler, you may want to choose to build some or most of the standard types and functions on your current installation. Combined with the portability practices outlined in Chapter 10, this approach will save a lot of time and will ease the stress of converting to standard C. In the following description of header files we attempt to point out how some of the standard features can be provided. The suggestions we make are not part of the standard and may therefore not be portable. Nevertheless, building even only some of the standard functions is in our opinion worth investigating. The investment will pay off in increased program portability and reduced conversion effort once the standard compiler is available for the particular installation.

Finally, we are not giving a full and formal definition of all the functions, macros and types defined by the standard. For such a definition, consult your language manual. The description given is less formal, possibly more intuitive and does not specify all the details of the functions' behaviour, possible error conditions and return values. We have not provided descriptions of the following, less frequently used headers: *assert.h, setjmp.h* and *stdarg.h*.

**<errno.h>**

The header <errno.h> defines macros and variables facilitating error processing. All the macros are required to start with upper case *E*, be followed by an
upper case letter or a digit, and expand to distinct integral constants suitable
for use in *#if* preprocessing directives. According to the 1989 version of the
standard there were only two macros defined by the standard: **EDOM** and
**ERANGE**. You should expect, however, that your installation defines many
more of them, if indeed it has the <errno.h> header file defined at all. Most
UNIX and MS-DOS compilers define a rich set of error constants describing
many possible failures of the library functions.

In addition to the error macros, the header defines a variable **errno**. The
variable is of type *int* and is set to a positive error number by many library
functions upon encountering an error condition. Although not explicitly
required by the standard, it should be expected that the value of this variable
will be equal to one of the error constants defined in the header.

A mechanism for retrieving a character string which describes the error is
mentioned in a subsequent section.

If the *errno.h* header is not defined on your system and if you decide to
provide one, it can easily be done by making sure that all your library
functions set *errno*. All possible error code values should then be defined in
the header.

**<stddef.h>**

The header <stddef.h> defines several types and macros considered to be
useful in most applications.

**ptrdiff_t**
> signed integral result of subtracting two pointers. It is typically
> defined to be a *long* and can be included in your own version of
> <stddef.h> on older compilers.

**size_t**
> unsigned integral result of the *sizeof* operator. It is typically defined
> to be *unsigned*.

**wchar_t**
> integral type which can represent codes for the entire, possibly
> extended character set. It is typically defined to be *char*.

**NULL**
> implementation defined null pointer constant. It is typically defined
> to be *0* or *0L*.

**offsetof(type, member)**

integral constant of type *size_t* representing an offset in bytes to the structure member *member* from the beginning of the structure *type*. It can be implemented by the following definition:

```
(size_t)&(((type*)0)->member)
```

## <ctype.h>

The header <ctype.h> declares functions used for testing and converting characters. All the testing functions can easily be implemented with a table driven approach, in which a static array containing bit masks for various character types is built. The array is indexed by the actual integer value of the character code, and the mask thus found indicates what is the type of the character. All classification functions in <ctype.h> return non-zero (true) if the character is of the type inquired about, zero (false) otherwise.

*Classification Functions*

| | |
|---|---|
| int isalnum(int c); | true if the argument is either a letter or a digit. |
| int isalpha(int c); | true if the argument is a letter. |
| int iscntrl(int c); | true if the argument is a control character. |
| int isdigit(int c); | true if the argument is a digit. |
| int isgraph(int c); | true if the argument is any printing character except space. |
| int islower(int c); | true if the argument is a lowercase letter. |
| int isprint(int c); | true if the argument is any printing character including space. |
| int ispunct(int c); | true if the argument is any printing character other than space, letter or digit. |
| int isspace(int c); | true if the argument is any white space character. |
| int isupper(int c); | true if the argument is an uppercase letter. |
| int isxdigit(int c); | true if the argument is a hexadecimal digit. |

*Translation Functions*

    int tolower(int c);          converts an uppercase letter to a corresponding lowercase letter.

    int toupper(int c);         converts a lowercase letter to a corresponding uppercase letter.

## <locale.h>

The header <locale.h> contains several macros and a type describing formatting rules for numeric values. It is intended to enable implementations to provide "internationalisation", that is, output formatting capabilities depending on the location of a particular C implementation. The structure defined in the header file defines, among others, characters to be used as a decimal point, thousands separator and currency symbols. The two corresponding library functions provide a means of setting the locale and extracting the symbols in the form of a pointer to a structure. The functions and the type can be easily provided in nonstandard environments by simply defining the structure according to the implementation's locale and defining the functions. In the simplest implementation, only one native "C" locale can be provided.

## <math.h>

The header <math.h> defines mathematical, floating point functions. All functions defined in this header take *double* values as their arguments and return *double* results. Most functions defined in this header can probably be found on your system. All of them are very difficult to implement and the implementation is typically very strongly machine dependent. In some environments, most notably in the MS-DOS environment, several versions of the functions may be defined depending on a system configuration. One version may use a floating point processor, another may emulate it, yet another may provide a simplified and faster version of the routines in which results may be guaranteed to be accurate only to a specified number of decimal places, or some nonstandard rounding may occur. If any of the functions given below is not available on your system and you are not intimately familiar with numerical analysis, nor have access to somebody who is, floating point libraries for your machine can probably be purchased from third party vendors. All trigonometric functions in the following list take or return angles in radians.

*Trigonometric Functions*

    **double acos (double x);**
        returns a principal value of the arc cosine of $x$.

    **double asin (double x);**
        returns a principal value of the arc sine of $x$.

    **double atan (double x);**
        returns a principal value of the arc tangent of $x$.

    **double atan2 (double x, double y);**
        returns a principal value of the arc tangent of $x/y$, using the signs of
        the two arguments to determine the quadrant of the result.

| | |
|---|---|
| **double cos (double x);** | returns the cosine of $x$. |
| **double sin (double x);** | returns the sine of $x$. |
| **double tan (double x);** | returns the tangent of $x$. |

*Hyperbolic Function*

| | |
|---|---|
| **double cosh (double x);** | returns the hyperbolic cosine of $x$. |
| **double sinh (double x);** | returns the hyperbolic sine of $x$. |
| **double tanh (double x);** | returns the hyperbolic tangent of $x$. |

*Logarithmic Functions*

    **double exp (double x);**
        returns the exponential function of $x$.

    **double frexp (double x, int \*exp);**
        returns the normalised fraction of $x$, and sets *exp* to an integer such
        that $x$ is equal to the result multiplied by 2 raised to the power \**exp*.
        In other words, the function breaks a number into a normalised
        fraction, that is a fraction from an interval [0.5, 1), and an integral
        power of 2. This directly corresponds to a standard IEEE internal
        representation of floating point numbers.

    **double ldexp (double x, int exp);**
        returns the value of $x$ times 2 raised to the power *exp*. It is the
        opposite of *frexp*.

double log (double x);
  returns the natural logarithm of $x$.

double log10 (double x);
  returns the base 10 logarithm of $x$.

double modf (double x, double *i);
  returns the signed fractional part of $x$ and sets $*i$ to a signed integral
  part of $x$.

*Power Functions*

double pow (double x, double y);
  returns the value of $x$ raised to the power $y$.

double sqrt (double x);
  returns the square root of $x$.

*Other Mathematical Functions*

double ceil (double x);
  returns the smallest integer not less than $x$.
double fabs (double x);
  returns the absolute value of $x$.
double floor (double x);
  returns the largest integer not greater than $x$.
double fmod (double x, double y);
  returns the remainder of $x/y$.

## <signal.h>

The header <signal.h> defines types, macros and functions dealing with
processing of various signals and conditions which may be reported asyn-
chronously during program execution. Such conditions may be the results of
errors or actions performed by the underlying operating system outside of the
domain of the program. Most C implementations define the header and the
corresponding functions. If it is not available on your implementation, you
must be intimately familiar with the operating system running on your
machine. In most cases, you must also be familiar with the hardware. Once
that knowledge is gained, the implementation itself is a relatively straightforward process consisting of recognizing hardware and software interrupts and

hooking them up to appropriate functions. For example, Intel processors starting with i286 support the *BOUND* instruction which can be used to check if an index used to access an array is within the array's bounds. If the check fails, the processor generates interrupt 5 which can be intercepted and used to generate a signal, which in turn can be captured by the application. Similarly, the *Ctrl-C* key combination is typically used to interrupt a program's execution. A software interrupt is generated (interrupt 0x1b under MS-DOS) which can be intercepted by the application.

The header file defines one type **sig_atomic_t**, an integral object which can be accessed as an atomic entity even in the presence of asynchronous events. It also defines the following macros each of which expands to an integral constant:

| | |
|---|---|
| **SIGABRT** | abnormal termination |
| **SIGFPE** | erroneous arithmetic operation |
| **SIGILL** | illegal instruction |
| **SIGINT** | interactive attention signal such as *Ctrl-C* |
| **SIGSEGV** | invalid access to storage |
| **SIGTERM** | termination request sent to the program |

The function defined in the header file allows the application to specify a signal handler. The handler will receive control whenever the specified condition occurs:

```
void (*signal (int sig, void (*func)(int))) (int);
```

The handler specified by *func* can be an application provided function, or can be **SIG_DFL** to instruct the system that an implementation defined default action is to be performed, or **SIG_IGN** to instruct the system that the signal should be ignored. If the call to *signal* succeeds it returns the most recent value of *func* for the signal, otherwise it returns **SIG_ERR**.

### <stdio.h>

The header <stdio.h> defines types, macros and functions for performing input and output. All C implementations have some form of this header file defined. Since input and output operations are very tightly coupled to the underlying operating system and hardware, good knowledge of the platform on which the implementation is supposed to run is required in order to be able to provide additional input/output functions. For example, a good knowledge of MS-DOS and BIOS is required to write any of the <stdio.h> functions on the PC family of computers. Similarly, knowledge of input/output related system calls and some knowledge of the kernel is needed to provide <stdio.h> library functions under the UNIX system.

The most often used constant defined in the <stdio.h> header is EOF which expands to a negative integer indicating end of file. It is returned by several functions to signal that no more input is available. The most important type defined in the header is FILE which defines an object which can contain all information pertaining to a file and allowing the application to control it, such as position information, buffer information and error indicators. The header also contains definitions of **stdin**, **stdout** and **stderr**, which are of type pointer to *FILE* and point to standard input, output and error files respectively. The three files are automatically opened at the beginning of any application.

## Operations on Files

The functions in this section operate on entire files and perform functions such as renaming or deletion of files.

> **int remove (const char \*name);**
>> causes the file given by *name* to be no longer accessible by that name. Please note that the standard does not require that file be physically removed.

> **int rename (const char \*oldname, const char \*newname);**
>> changes the name of a file from *oldname* to *newname*.

> **FILE \*tmpfile (void);**
>> creates and opens for update a temporary file which will automatically be closed and removed at program termination.

> **char \*tmpnam (char \*s);**
>> generates a temporary file name, that is a valid file name different from any other existing file.

## File Access Functions

The functions in this section provide means for applications to access the files. This is done by establishing a logical connection between an external stream and the file pointer internal to the application.

> **int fclose (FILE \*stream);**
>> the file is flushed and closed. The connection between the file pointer and an external stream is broken.

**int fflush (FILE *stream);**
> if *stream* points to a file on which the last operation was not input, the function will cause all buffered data to be written. For efficiency, most file operations are buffered. This function flushes the buffers.

**FILE *fopen (const char *name, cons char *mode);**
> opens a file given by *name* in a mode given by *mode*. The mode specifies if the file is read only, read and write, and what should be the initial value of the file position indicator.

**FILE *freopen (const char *name, const char *mode, FILE *stream);**
> closes the file given by *stream* and then opens a file given by *name* and associates it with *stream*.

**void setvbuf (FILE *stream, char *buf, int mode, size_t size);**
> the function can only be used right after opening a file before performing any other operation on it. *mode* indicates the type of buffering to be performed, *buf* points to a buffer which may be used for buffering, and *size* specifies the size of the buffer.

*Formatted Input and Output*

The functions in this section perform formatted input and output. As described in Chapter 3, formatted input and output functions in C provide a very rich repertoire of conversions and formatting options. The format strings are interpreted at runtime, thus providing the flexibility of dynamically building the format strings.

**int fprintf (FILE *stream, const char *format, ...);**
> performs formatted write to a file. This function has been discussed in detail in Chapter 3.

**int fscanf (FILE *stream, const char *format, ...);**
> performs formatted read from a file. This function has been discussed in detail in Chapter 3.

**int printf (const char *format, ...);**
> is equivalent to *fprintf* with *stdout* specified for *stream*.

**int scanf (const char *format, ...);**
> is equivalent to *fscanf* with *stdin* specified for *stream*.

```
int sprintf (char *buf, const char *format, ...);
```
is equivalent to *fprintf* except that the output is written to character array *buf*, not to a file.

```
int sscanf (const char *buf, const char *format, ...);
```
is equivalent to *fscanf* except that the input is read from character array *buf*, not from a file.

## Character Input and Output

The functions in this section provide a string or a single character input and output capabilities.

```
int fgetc (FILE *stream);
```
gets the next character from a file, or *EOF* if the file is at an end.

```
char *fgets (char *s, int n, FILE *stream);
```
reads at most *n-1* characters from the file *stream* and puts them into character array *s*. The function will not read past a new-line character or an end of file. The string read is terminated by a null character. The function returns the address of string *s*, or *EOF* on failure.

```
int fputc (int c, FILE *stream);
```
places character *c* in the file *stream* and advances the file position indicator so that the next call to *putc* places the character at the next position.

```
char *fputs (const char *s, FILE *stream);
```
writes characters from the string *s* to the file *stream* at the current file position and advances the file position indicator accordingly. The terminating null character is not written.

```
int getc (FILE *stream);
```
is equivalent to *fgetc* but is implemented as a macro. The argument may be evaluated more than once.

```
int getchar (void);
```
is equivalent to *getc* with the argument *stream* equal to *stdin*.

**char \*gets (char \*s);**

    behaves like *fgets* with the argument *stream* equal to stdin. Please note, however, that the maximum number of characters to be read cannot be specified. The function always reads until a new line character or an end of file is encountered and can thus be used only if the maximum record size can be guaranteed.

**int putc (int c, FILE \*stream);**

    is equivalent to *fputc* but is implemented as a macro. The *stream* argument can be evaluated more than once and therefore cannot be an expression with side effects.

**int putchar (int c);**

    is equivalent to *putc* with the argument *stream* equal to *stdout*.

**int puts (const char \*s);**

    behaves like *fputs* with the argument *stream* equal to *stdout*. In addition, a new line character is appended to the output for each string written.

**int ungetc (int c, FILE \*stream);**

    pushes the character *c* back onto the file *stream*. The character will be returned by subsequent reads on the file, but the external, physical image of the file is not changed, so this function is not equivalent to writing to the file. Repositioning of the file discards any characters pushed onto it using this call. The standard guarantees at least one level of push. Subsequent calls to this function may fail, in which case *EOF* is returned.

*Direct Input and Output*

The functions in this section provide unformatted, direct input and output. They read and write objects of arbitrary size and structure.

**size_t fread (void \*buf, size_t size, size_t num, FILE \*stream);**

    reads *num* elements each of size *size* from the file *stream* and places them in the area of storage pointed to by *buf*. The function returns the number of elements read, which may be less than *num* if an error or an end of file is encountered.

size_t fwrite (const void *buf, size_t size, size_t num, FILE
*stream);

> writes *num* elements each of size *size* to the file *stream*. The objects
> are taken from the area of storage pointed to by *buf*. The function
> returns the number of elements written, which may be less than *num*
> if an error is encountered.

## File Positioning

The functions in this section provide means to inquire about and change the
file position indicators.

int fgetpos (FILE *stream, fpos_t *pos);

> stores the current value of the file position indicator for file *stream*
> in the variable pointed to by *pos*. The type and format of the
> information stored in *pos* is not specified by the standard.

int fsetpos (FILE *stream, const fpos_t *pos);

> sets the current value of the file position indicator for file *stream* to
> the position specified in the variable pointed to by *pos*. The value of
> *pos* is obtained from a previous call to *fgetpos*. Please note that the
> *fgetpos* and *fsetpos* pair provide means to store the current file
> position and then go back to that position after intervening read and
> write calls.

int fseek (FILE *stream, long offset, int whence);

> sets the file position indicator to *offset* characters from the position
> specified by *whence*. *whence* can be SEEK_SET to indicate the
> beginning of the file, SEEK_CUR to indicate the current position,
> or SEEK_END to indicate an end of file. The standard does not
> require that SEEK_END be supported.

long ftell (FILE *stream);

> returns the current value of the file position indicator for file
> *stream.*

void rewind (FILE *stream);

> is equivalent to *(void)fseek (stream, 0L, SEEK_SET);* and clears any
> errors on the file.

*Error Handling*

All input and output functions can generate errors. The functions in this section operate on the error indicators set by other input and output functions.

**void clearerr (FILE \*stream);**

clears end of file and error conditions for *stream*.

**int feof (FILE \*stream);**

tests if *stream* is at the end of file. Returns true (non-zero) if such is the case, zero otherwise.

**int ferror (FILE \*stream);**

returns true (non-zero) if the error indicator is set for *stream*.

**void perror (const char \*s);**

writes an error message to *stderr*. The error message consists of a string pointed to by *s*, followed by an implementation defined error message corresponding to the value of the global variable *errno*.

# <stdlib.h>

The header <stdlib.h> defines types, macros and functions considered to be of general utility. The contents of this header file have evolved over a period of several years and were standardized by the ANSI standard. Some or most of the functions may be present on your implementation. Many of the functions in this header file, such as string conversion functions, can be implemented with relative ease. Memory allocation functions may be more challenging and will require understanding of memory management techniques employed by the target operating system. Sorting, searching and random number generating functions are almost classical examples of basic computer science exercises and can be found in every book on computing. Finally, functions dealing with process termination are intricately woven into the basic fabric of the operating system.

*String Conversions*

The functions in this section convert strings to numbers. The standard provides a detailed discussion of the behaviour of these functions. The most important characteristic of this behaviour is the fact that the functions are highly error tolerant. The strings passed to the conversion functions can contain leading blank space, and the number sequence can be followed by other, non-numeric and unrecognised characters. The sequence of digits embedded in the string is referred to as a subject sequence, and is defined as a longest initial subsequence of the input string that is of a form expected for the given type of conversion. The part of the string that remains is referred to below as the "final string".

**double strtod (const char \*inptr, char \*\*outptr);**
> converts the subject sequence in *inptr* to *double* representation. A pointer to the final string is stored in *outptr*, provided that *outptr* is not *NULL*.

**long strtol (const char \*inptr, char \*\*outptr, int base);**
> converts the subject sequence in *inptr* to *long* representation. A pointer to the final string is stored in *outptr*, provided that *outptr* is not *NULL*. *base* specifies the base of conversion. Letters from "a" (or "A") to "z" (or "Z") are assigned values from 10 to 35. Only letters with assigned values of less than *base* are permitted in the subject sequence. If base is 16, a sequence "0x" or "0X" may optionally precede the subject sequence.

**unsigned long strtoul (const char \*inptr, char \*\*outptr, int base);**
> converts the subject sequence in *inptr* to *unsigned long* representation. A pointer to the final string is stored in *outptr*, provided that *outptr* is not *NULL*. *base* specifies the base of conversion. Letters from "a" (or "A") to "z" (or "Z") are assigned values from 10 to 35. Only letters with assigned values of less than *base* are permitted in the subject sequence. If base is 16, a sequence "0x" or "0X" may optionally precede the subject sequence.

**int atoi (const char \*inptr);**
> behaves like *(int)strtol (inptr, (char \*\*)NULL, 10);*.

**long atol (const char \*inptr);**
> behaves like *strtol (inptr, (char \*\*)NULL, 10);*.

*Pseudo Random Number Generation*

**int rand (void);**
> returns a pseudo random integer in the range 0 to **RAND_MAX**. *RAND_MAX* has to be at least 32767.

**void srand (unsigned seed);**
> uses *seed* as a beginning of a new pseudo random sequence.

The ANSI standard provides a portable implementation for these two functions as follows:

```
static unsigned long int next = 1;

int rand (void)
{
    /* RAND_MAX is assumed to be 32767 */
    next = next * 1103515245 + 12345;
    return ((unsigned int)(next / 65536) % 32768);

} /* rand */

void srand (unsigned int seed)
{
    next = seed;

    return;

} /* srand */
```

*Memory Management*

Memory management functions are at the heart of complex data structures in all but the most trivial applications. We have seen how the memory management functions are used in example 9.3. Large and complex applications will typically rely heavily on the memory management functions, and mishandling of memory management is the source of some of the most common and most difficult to find C programming errors.

Memory is said to be allocated from a memory pool called a heap. The operating system manages all system resources and allocates memory to individual processes (programs) as requested and as available. The standard C library maintains the individual heap allocated to the process by the operating system. Individual pieces of the heap are given to the application as a result of *malloc* calls, and are returned to the heap by *free*. It is up to the application to free all the pieces of storage requested via *malloc*, or else all space in the heap may be exhausted. Should that happen, the reaction to subsequent memory allocation requests varies from system to system. Simple operating systems with limited resources, such as MS-DOS with its memory limitations, may allocate the entire system memory to be used by a single process. Running out of heap space is in those cases equivalent to running out of the entire system memory, in which case the *malloc* call returns an error and there is very little else that the application can do, unless of course it can return some memory to the free pool by calling *free*. In sophisticated operating systems, such as the UNIX system, the memory management library functions may request that the heap space available to the process be increased. The system, having virtual memory capabilities, often honours such requests practically indefinitely. The address space of the process grows and places huge demands on the system, bringing it slowly to a grinding halt.

The most fundamental rule for using dynamic memory management in C is to free all the space allocated. Many development environments provide various functions and utilities to check the heap and make sure that the space which has not been allocated is not used by the application. It is, however, entirely up to the programmer to make sure that whatever has been allocated is freed when no longer needed.

**void \*malloc (size_t size);**
> allocates space for an object of size *size* and returns a pointer to the space allocated or *NULL* if the request fails. The content of the allocated space is indeterminate.

**void free (void \*ptr);**
> deallocates space pointed to by *ptr*. If *ptr* is *NULL*, no action occurs. If *ptr* points to an object that has not been previously allocated, or has been deallocated since, the behaviour is undefined.

**void \*calloc (size_t num, size_t size);**
> allocates space for *num* objects of size *size* each, sets the space allocated to all zeros and returns a pointer to the space allocated or *NULL* if the request fails.

**void \*realloc (void \*ptr, size_t size);**
> changes size of the object pointed to by *ptr* to *size*. The content of the object is unchanged up to the lesser of the old and new size. The function essentially behaves like a series of *malloc*, followed by *memcpy*, followed by *free* of the old space. The function returns a pointer to the new memory area.

## Communication with the Environment

The functions in this section provide means to examine the environment and return results of the program operation to the underlying operating system.

**void abort (void);**
> causes abnormal program termination by raising signal *SIGABRT* and exiting the application (unless the signal is caught).

**int atexit (void (\*func)(void));**
> specifies that the function *func* is to be called at normal program termination. Multiple functions can be specified by multiple calls to *atexit*. The standard guarantees support of at least 32 such functions.

**void exit (int status);**
> normally terminates the program, calls all functions specified by *atexit* (in the reverse order), flushes and closes all files and returns *status* to the host environment.

**char \*getenv (const char \*name);**
> searches the environment for a string specified by *name* and returns a pointer to a string associated with the name or *NULL* if the name cannot be found.

**int system (const char \*command);**
> passes the *command* to the command processor of the host environment and returns an implementation defined value.

*Searching and Sorting*

**void qsort (void \*base, size_t num, size_t size, int (\*compar)(const void \*, const void\*));**
> sorts an array of *num* objects each of size *size*. The first object in the array is pointed to by *base* and the comparison function is provided by the application and given in *compar*. The comparison function will be passed two pointers to the elements to be compared and must return an integer less than, equal to or greater than 0, depending on whether the first argument is less than, equal to or greater than the second.

**void \*bsearch (const void \*key, const void \*base, size_t num size_t size, int (\*compar)(const void \*, const void\*));**
> performs a binary search on an array of *num* objects each of size *size*. The first object in the array is pointed to by *base* and the comparison function is provided by the application and given in *compar*. The comparison function will be passed a pointer to the *key* object and an array element and must return an integer less than, equal to or greater than 0, depending on whether the key is less than, equal to or greater than the array element. The function returns a pointer to the matching array element or *NULL*.

## <string.h>

The header <string.h> defines types, macros and functions dealing with operations on arrays of characters. The functions fall into two main categories. Functions whose names start with *mem* are not sensitive to the content of the character strings operated on and can thus be used to operate on arbitrary objects. Functions whose names start with *str* assume that the objects are null terminated character strings and may terminate their operation upon encountering the null character. All functions defined in this header can be easily written in C even if not available on your installation. Many of them have been specified in the original K&R language definition.

*Copying*

> **void \*memcpy (void \*dest, const void \*src, size_t n);**
>> copies *n* characters from *src* to *dest*. If the areas pointed to by *src* and *dest* overlap, the behaviour is undefined. The function returns the pointer to the destination object.

> **void \*memmove (void \*dest, const void \*src, size_t n);**
>> copies *n* characters from *src* to *dest*. The function works correctly for overlapping areas of storage and returns the pointer to the destination object.

> **char \*strcpy (void \*dest, const void \*src);**
>> copies characters from *src* to *dest* strings including the terminating *NULL* character. If the areas pointed to by *src* and *dest* overlap, the behaviour is undefined. The function returns the pointer to the destination string.

> **char \*strncpy (void \*dest, const void \*src, size_t n);**
>> copies at most *n* characters from *src* to *dest* strings including the terminating *NULL* character. If the areas pointed to by *src* and *dest* overlap, the behaviour is undefined. The function returns the pointer to the destination string.

*Concatenation*

> **char \*strcat (void \*dest, const void \*src);**
>> appends characters from *src* to *dest* strings including the terminating *NULL* character. If the areas pointed to by *src* and *dest* overlap, the behaviour is undefined. The function returns the pointer to the destination string.

> **char \*strncat (void \*dest, const void \*src, size_t n);**
>> appends at most *n* characters from *src* to *dest* strings including the terminating *NULL* character. If the areas pointed to by *src* and *dest* overlap, the behaviour is undefined. The function returns the pointer to the destination string.

## Comparison

**int strcmp (const char \*s1, const char \*s2);**
> compares characters from *s1* to characters from *s2*. Returns an integer less than, equal to, or greater than zero if the object pointed to by *s1* is less than, equal to or greater than object pointed to by *s2*.

**int strncmp (const char \*s1, const char \*s2, size_t n);**
> compares at most *n* characters from *s1* to characters from *s2*. Returns an integer less than, equal to, or greater than zero if the string pointed to by *s1* is less than, equal to or greater than string pointed to by *s2*.

**int memcmp (const void \*s1, const void \*s2, size_t n);**
> compares *n* characters from *s1* to characters from *s2*. Returns an integer less than, equal to, or greater than zero if the object pointed to by *s1* is less than, equal to or greater than objectpointed to by *s2*.

## Searching

**void \*memchr (const void \*s, int c, size_t n);**
> returns a pointer to the first occurrence of a character given by *c* in the first *n* characters of an object pointed to by *s*, or returns *NULL* if the character does not occur in the object.

**char \*strchr (const char \*s, int c);**
> returns a pointer to the first occurrence of a character given by *c* in the string pointed to by *s*, or returns *NULL* if the character does not occur in the string.

**char \*strrchr (const char \*s, int c);**
> returns a pointer to the last occurrence of a character given by *c* in the string pointed to by *s*, or returns *NULL* if the character does not occur in the string.

**size_t strspn (const char \*s1, const char \*s2);**
> returns the length of the maximum initial segment of the string *s1* which consists entirely of characters from *s2*.

**size_t strcspn (const char \*s1, const char \*s2);**
> returns the length of the maximum initial segment of the string *s1* which consists entirely of characters not from *s2*.

**char \*strpbrk (const char \*s1, const char \*s2);**
> returns a pointer to the first occurrence in *s1* of any character from *s2*.

**char \*strstr (const char \*s1, const char \*s2);**
> returns a pointer to the first occurrence in *s1* of a sequence of characters in *s2*.

**char \*strtok (const char \*s1, const char \*s2);**
> breaks the string *s1* into tokens delimited by any of the characters specified in *s2*. Returns a pointer to the first character of a token or *NULL* if there are no tokens left. The function is intended to be used in a series of calls. The first call passes the address of the first character string *s1*. Subsequent calls are made with the first argument set to *NULL* to indicate that the same initial string is to be parsed. It is expected that a series of tokens is returned and a null pointer is returned on the last call when all the tokens are parsed.

*Miscellaneous*

**size_t strlen (const char \*s);**
> returns the length of the string pointed to by *s*.

**void \*memset (void \*s, int c, size_t n);**
> places the value *c* into the first *n* characters of the object pointed to by *s* and returns *s*.

**char \*strerror (int errnum);**
> converts an error code in *errnum* to an implementation defined error message.

**<time.h>**

The header <time.h> defines types, macros and functions dealing with operations on time values. The types are: **clock_t** and **time_t** typically defined to be *long*, and a structure holding the components of a calendar time. The structure is defined as follows:

```
struct tm {
    int   tm_sec;     /* seconds after the minute [0,61]
                                          (leap seconds) */
    int   tm_min;     /* minutes after the hour [0,59] */
    int   tm_hour;    /* hours since midnight [0,23] */
    int   tm_mday;    /* day of the month [1,31] */
    int   tm_mon;     /* months since January [0,11] */
    int   tm_year;    /* years since 1900 */
    int   tm_wday;    /* days since Sunday [0,6] */
    int   tm_yday;    /* days since January 1st [0,365] */
    int   tm_isdst;   /* daylight saving time flag */
};
```

In addition, the **CLOCKS_PER_SEC** macro is defined and specifies the number of system clock ticks per second. For example, the value of this macro on MS-DOS machines is 18.2.

## Time Manipulation

**clock_t clock (void);**
> returns the number of system clock ticks since the beginning of the application. The standard only talks about "best approx-imation", therefore, in order to obtain the amount of time spent in an application, the current value of *clock* should be decreased by the value obtained at the beginning of a program.

**time_t time (time_t *timer);**
> retrieve the system's current calendar time. The encoding of the value returned is not specified but it must be suitable for use by other functions in the "time" family.

**double difftime (time_t t1, time_t t0);**
> returns a difference in seconds between *t1* and *t0*.

## Time Conversions

**time_t mktime (struct tm *timeptr);**
> converts the broken down time in structure *timeptr* to a calendar time value in the same form as the one returned from the *time* function. The values in various element of the time structure are not limited to the ranges given above, but rather are recalculated and adjusted accordingly so that they fall into the ranges upon the function return.

**struct tm *localtime (const time_t *timer);**
> converts the calendar time given in *timer* to a broken down time format and returns values expressed in the local time zone.

**struct tm *gmtime (const time_t *timer);**
> converts the calendar time given in *timer* to a broken down time format and returns values expressed as Coordinated Universal Time (GMT).

**char *asctime (const struct tm *timeptr);**
> returns a pointer to a string containing a printable representation of the time contained in structure *time*. The string is of the form: *"Fri Aug 21 14:03:52 1981\n\0"*.

char \*ctime (const time_t \*timer);
   equivalent to *asctime(localtime(timer))*

size_t strftime (char \*s, size_t maxsize, const char \*format, const struct tm \*timeptr);

   places a character representation of the time given in *timeptr* into a character string pointed to by *s*. No more than *maxsize* characters are placed in the string and the conversion is governed by the *format* string. The function behaves like *sprintf* but operates on the time structure rather than arbitrary data values. The *format* string contains character strings conversion specifiers. The character strings are placed in *s* verbatim and the conversion specifiers are replaced by the corresponding values as follows:

| | |
|---|---|
| %a | abbreviated weekday name (locale specific) |
| %A | full weekday name (locale specific) |
| %b | abbreviated month name (locale specific) |
| %B | full month name (locale specific) |
| %c | date and time representation (locale specific) |
| %d | day of the month [1-31] |
| %H | hour of the day [00-23] |
| %I | hour of the day [01-12] |
| %j | day of the year [001-366] |
| %m | month of the year [01-12] |
| %M | minute of the hour [00-59] |
| %p | AM/PM designation (locale specific) |
| %S | seconds [00-61] (up to two leap seconds) |
| %U | week of the year [00-53] (first Sunday as the first day of week 1) |
| %w | weekday [0-6] - Sunday=0 |
| %W | week of the year [00-53] (first Monday as the first day of week 1) |
| %x | date representation (locale specific) |
| %X | time representation (locale specific) |
| %y | year without century [00-99] |
| %Y | year with century |
| %z | time zone name |
| %% | % |

## Summary

In contrast with many other modern programming languages, the original C definition did not specify any built-in functions. The emphasis has been on the language simplicity and power typically associated with lower level languages such as assembler. However, over the years of usage and popularity of C, a set of *de facto* standard functions provided in a form of a library on most C installations has evolved. The definitions of most of these functions have been formalised, additional functions have been provided and the set is now part of the ANSI standard, in the sense that any implementation claiming to be standard must provide them. Even if your installation is not yet standard, you should probably expect it to convert soon. It is advisable to ease the stress of converting to a different flavour of C by careful planning. Providing some of the standard functions ahead of time, together with applying portability techniques outlined in Chapter 10, will prove to be a good investment.

# Appendix 1: C Style Analysis

The features of a program that contribute to its 'elegance' are very much subjective, and often instinctive. A superficial analysis of a program's 'style' (that is, its visual presentation), while not being the only factor, is certainly an indicative, and easily automated, component.

Presented here is a program that performs a textual analysis of a C program, yielding a percentage 'style score'. The code is also available on a floppy diskette - see the Introduction for details.

## STYLE ANALYSIS

The features that contribute to the style score are based on proposals made by Rees (1982), adapted for C rather than Pascal:

| | |
|---|---|
| Module length | The average length, in non-blank lines, of function definitions; functions that are prolific and too short tend to obscure the program logic, while those that are too long are difficult to dismember. |
| Identifier length | The average length, in characters, of user identifiers; brief identifier names (such as *i* or *c*) are often meaningless, while overlong names make the program verbose (most programmers will know that selection of pithy, meaningful identifier names is often one of the most time consuming elements of writing code). |
| Comments | The percentage of all lines that contain comments; over-commenting is as much a sin as under-commenting; some comments, however, are always necessary, even in the shortest of programs. |
| Indentation | The ratio of initial spaces to total number of characters; indentation can be used to good effect to indicate the program structure. |
| Blank lines | The percentage of all lines that are blank; blank lines |

separate functional units of a program.

Line length
: The average number of non-blank characters per line; sensible use of multiple-statement lines can make a program visually concise, but not obscure.

Embedded spaces
: The average number of embedded spaces per line; embedded spaces do for a line what blank lines do for a function.

Constant definitions
: The percentage of all user identifiers that are defined constants; use of manifest constants not only makes a program easier to modify, it also associates meaning with a constant.

Reserved words
: The number of different reserved words and standard functions used; the variety of reserved words used is indicative of command of the language.

Included files
: The extent to which a program is segmented by using *#include* files; breaking constant definitions, macros and type definitions out into shared header files reduces program complexity.

Goto statements
: The number of occurrences of a *goto* statement; advocates of structured programming will usually allow the use of a single *goto* in a program to handle a special exit condition - more than that is a cardinal sin!

A score is associated with each of the above metrics, each contributing a different maximum percentage to the final score, in recognition of the fact that some factors are more important than others. All scores are additive, with the exception of the last, which is subtractive. Too high or too low a figure for each metric is detrimental to the final score.

The individual score is determined by reference to a table which specifies, for each metric (shown graphically in table A1.1):

Table A1.1

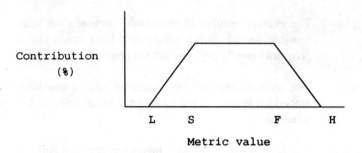

- the point L, below which no score is obtained;
- the point S, the start of the 'ideal range' for the metric;
- the point F, the finish of the ideal range; and
- the point H, above which no score is obtained.

Values between S and F score maximum marks; those between L and S, and F and H, score marks depending on their exact position within the range.

## THE STYLE PROGRAM

```c
#include <stdio.h>
#include <ctype.h>

/* When dividing, use this to prevent division by zero */
#define RDIV(d,v)    ((v) ? (double) (d) / (double) (v) : 0.0)

/* This macro is useful to find the number of elements
   in a static structure array */
#define ELEMENTS_IN(x)   (sizeof(x) / sizeof(x[0]))

/* This structure holds the title and value of
   the measured quantities */
#define MQ(x)    { x, 0 }
static struct {
    char *title;
    int value;
} stats[] = {
    MQ("Blank lines           "),
    MQ("Total lines           "),
    MQ("Total characters      "),
    MQ("Indented spaces       "),
    MQ("Embedded spaces       "),
    MQ("Nonblank characters   "),
    MQ("Comment lines         "),
    MQ("Include lines         "),
    MQ("Define lines          "),
    MQ("Modules               "),
    MQ("Goto's                "),
    MQ("Reserved word variety"),
    MQ("Non-reserved words    ")
};
```

```c
/* These serve as indexes into the measured
   quantities array (stats) */
#define BLANK_LINES       0
#define TOTAL_LINES       1
#define TOTAL_CHARS       2
#define INDENT_SPACES     3
#define EMBEDDED_SPACES   4
#define NONBLANK_CHARS    5
#define COMMENT_LINES     6
#define INCLUDE_LINES     7
#define DEFINE_LINES      8
#define MODULES           9
#define GOTOS             10
#define RESWORD_VARIETY   11
#define NONRESWORDS       12

/* This structure will hold state information across
   lines of input. Thus, we can keep track of whether
   we are in the middle of a multi-line comment,
   preprocessor directive, identifier, constant,
   or structure declaration */
struct _state {
    char in_comment, in_define, in_include,
         in_string_const, in_char_const,
         in_identifier, in_num_const,
         in_struct_dec;
};

/* This structure (with the add_char routine) allows
   identifiers and lines to have unrestricted lengths */
static struct _buf {
    int index;
    char *chars;
    unsigned size;
} line, identifier;

/* Pointer to the character in the line which
   is being examined */
static char *lineptr;

/* This structure implements a forward singly
   linked list of user identifiers */
static struct _user_ident {
    struct _user_ident *next;
    char name[1];
} *first_user_ident;

/* Current level, incremented at every "{",
   decremented at every "}" */
static int level = 0;

/* The list of reserved words is kept here */
#define RW(x)    { x, 0 }
static struct {
    char *identifier;
    int used;
} reserved_words[] = {
RW("auto"),      RW("break"),     RW("case"),      RW("char"),
RW("const"),     RW("continue"),  RW("default"),   RW("do"),
RW("double"),    RW("else"),      RW("enum"),      RW("extern"),
RW("float"),     RW("for"),       RW("goto"),      RW("if"),
RW("int"),       RW("long"),      RW("register"),  RW("return"),
RW("short"),     RW("signed"),    RW("sizeof"),    RW("static"),
RW("struct"),    RW("switch"),    RW("typedef"),   RW("union"),
RW("unsigned"),  RW("void"),      RW("volatile"),  RW("while")
};
```

```
/* Prototypes for ANSI conforming compilers */
#ifdef __STDC__
#define P(x)    x

/* List all external functions that do not return an int */
extern void exit (int), free (char *), perror (char *);
extern char *malloc (unsigned), *realloc (char *, unsigned),
    *strcpy (char *, char *);


#else
#define ASTR    *
#define P(x)    (/ASTR x ASTR/)


/* List all external functions that do not return an int */
extern void exit (), free (), perror ();
extern char *malloc (), *realloc (), *strcpy ();
#endif

/* Function prototypes */
static char add_char P((struct _buf *, char));
static void add_identifier P((char *));
static void expand_tab P((void));
static void free_identifiers P((void));
static int is_preprocess P((char *));
static int is_reserved P((char *));
int main P((int, char *[]));
static int parse_const P((char));
static int parse_ident P((void));
static void parse_line P((struct _state *));
static int parse_num_const P((void));
static void process_file P((FILE *));
static void process_line P((struct _state *));
static void process_stats P((void));

/* Add a character to a _buf structure.  Get more space
   if necessary */
static char
add_char (buf, c)
struct _buf *buf;
char c;
{
    int offset = lineptr - buf->chars;

    /* Check if more space is needed: if so, allocate it */
    if (buf index >= buf->size) {
        if ((buf->chars = realloc (buf->chars, buf->size *= 2))
                        == NULL) {
            fprintf (stderr, "Error allocating %d bytes\n",
                    buf->size);
            exit (1);
        }
        lineptr = buf->chars + offset;
    }

    /* Copy the character and return its value */
    return (buf->chars[buf->index++] = c);
}
```

```
/* Free the list of user identifiers */
static void
free_identifiers ()
{
    struct _user_ident *i = first_user_ident;

    /* Go through the list and free each identifier */
    while (i) {
        i = i->next;
        free (first_user_ident);
        first_user_ident = i;
    }

    /* Reset the first pointer to zero */
    first_user_ident = (struct _user_ident *) 0;
}


/* Add a user identifier to the forward singly linked list */
static void
add_identifier (ident)
char *ident;
{
    int j;
    struct _user_ident *i;

    /* If this identifier has already been entered,
       just return */
    for (i = first_user_ident; i; i = i->next)
        if (!strcmp (i->name, ident))
            return;

    /* Allocate space for the new _user_ident structure */
    if ((i = (struct _user_ident *)
            malloc (sizeof(i) + strlen (ident) + 1)) == NULL) {
        fprintf (stderr, "Error allocating %d bytes.\n",
                    sizeof(i) + strlen (ident) + 1);
        exit (1);
    }

    /* Copy the identifier in, link in the new _user_ident
       structure at the front of the list, update the
       non-reserved words count. */
    strcpy (i->name, ident);
    i->next = first_user_ident;
    first_user_ident = i;
    stats[NONRESWORDS].value++;
}


/* Check to see if this is a preprocessor directive */
static
is_preprocess (directive)
char *directive;
{
    int i;
    char c;

    /* Check for optional leading white space, then
       the character "#", then optional white space,
       and then the indicated directive. */
    for (i = 0; line.chars[i] && isspace(line.chars[i]); i++)
        ;
    if (line.chars[i++] != '#')
        return 0;
```

```
    while (line.chars[i] && isspace(line.chars[i]))
        i++;
    if (strncmp (directive, &line.chars[i],
                            strlen (directive)))
        return 0;

    /* Make sure the next character is not
       alphanumeric or " " */
    c = line.chars[i + strlen (directive)];
    if (isalnum(c) || c == '_')
        return 0;
    return 1;
}


/* Expand a tab to spaces */
static void
expand_tab ()
{
    int i;
    int offset = lineptr - line.chars;/* Location of tab */
    int add_spaces = 7 - offset % 8;  /* Number of spaces
                                                to add */

    /* Get more space if necessary */
    if (strlen (line.chars) + add_spaces + 1 > line.size) {
        if ((line.chars = realloc (line.chars,
                            line.size *= 2)) == NULL) {
            fprintf (stderr, "Error allocating %d bytes\n",
                                                line.size);
            exit (1);
        }
        lineptr = line.chars + offset;
    }

    /* Shift characters to make room for spaces */
    for (i = strlen (line.chars); i > offset; i--)
    line.chars[i + add_spaces] = line.chars[i];

    /* Fill in spaces */
    while (add_spaces >= 0)
        line.chars[offset + add_spaces--] = ' ';
}


/* Parse the input line, stripping out comments, figuring
   out where string constants, character constants,
   identifiers, and numeric constants are.  Also, expand
   tabs to spaces when not in constants. */
static void
parse_line (state)
struct _state *state;
{
    char *comment_start;    /* Pointer to start of comment */
    int comment_counted = 0, line_length;

    /* Loop through each character in the line */
    for (comment_start = lineptr = line.chars;
                                    *lineptr; lineptr++) {

        /* A comment was detected. */
        if (state->in_comment) {
            char *p, *q;

                /* Update statistics, if necessary */
```

```
if (!comment_counted) {
    comment_counted = 1;
    stats[COMMENT_LINES].value++;
}


/* Look for terminating comment symbol */
for ( ; *lineptr; lineptr++)
    if (*lineptr == '*' && *(lineptr+1) == '/') {
        state->in_comment = 0;
        lineptr += 2;
        break;
    }


/* Strip out comment by moving characters after
   the comment on top of where comment began */
for (p = lineptr, q = comment_start; *q++ = *p++;)
    ;


/* Reposition the pointer to the
   current character */
lineptr = comment_start - 1;


/* A string constant (e.g., "foo") was detected. */
} else if (state->in_string_const) {
    state->in_string_const = parse_const ('"');


/* A character constant (e.g., 'f') was detected. */
} else if (state->in_char_const) {
    state->in_char_const = parse_const ('\'');
/* An identifier was detected */
} else if (state->in_identifier) {
    state->in_identifier = parse_ident (state);


/* A numeric constant was detected */
} else if (state->in_num_const) {
    state->in_num_const = parse_num_const ();


/* If this is a tab, expand it to spaces */
} else if (*lineptr == '\t') {
    expand_tab ();


/* Check if this is the start of an identifier */
} else if (isalpha(*lineptr) || *lineptr == '_') {
    state->in_identifier = 1;
    (void) add_char (&identifier, *lineptr);


/* Check if this is the start of a number */
} else if (isdigit(*lineptr)) {
    state->in_num_const = parse_num_const ();


/* Check for preprocessor include's or define's */
} else if (*lineptr == '#') {
    if (is_preprocess ("include"))
        state->in_include = 1;
    else if (is_preprocess ("define"))
        state->in_define = 1;


/* Check if this is the start of a comment */
} else if (*lineptr == '/' && *(lineptr+1) == '*') {
    state->in_comment = 1;
    comment_start = lineptr++;
```

```
            /* Check if this is the start of a
               character constant */
            } else if (*lineptr == '\'') {
                state->in_char_const = 1;

            /* Check if this is the start of a
               string constant */
            } else if (*lineptr == '"') {
                state->in_string_const = 1;

            /* Check for function declaration - every time we
               encounter a "{", we bump the level, every time
               we encounter "}", we reduce it. If a "}" takes
               us to level 0, we've just reached the end of a
               structure or union declaration */
            } else if (*lineptr == '{') {
                if (!state->in_comment &&
                    !state->in_string_const &&
                    !state->in_char_const)
                    level++;
            } else if (*lineptr == ';') {
                if (state->in_struct_dec && level == 0)
                    state->in_struct_dec = 0;
            } else if (*lineptr == '}') {
                if (!state->in_comment &&
                    !state->in_string_const &&
                    !state->in_char_const)
                    if (--level == 0 &&
                        !state->in_struct_dec &&
                        !state->in_define)
                        stats[MODULES].value++;
            }
        }

    /* Update number of include line statistics */
    if (state->in_include) {
        stats[INCLUDE_LINES].value++;
        line_length = strlen (line.chars);
        if (line_length == 0 ||
            line.chars[line_length - 1] != '\\')
            state->in_char_const = state->in_string_const =
                state->in_include = state->in_comment =
                state->in_struct_dec = 0;

    /* Update number of define line statistics */
    } else if (state->in_define) {
        stats[DEFINE_LINES].value++;
        line_length = strlen (line.chars);
        if (line_length == 0 ||
            line.chars[line_length - 1] != '\\')
            state->in_char_const = state->in_string_const =
                state->in_define = state->in_comment =
                state->in_struct_dec = 0;
    }
}
```

```c
/* This routine is called once for each input line */
static void
process_line (state)
struct _state *state;
{
    int i;

    stats[TOTAL_LINES].value++;

    /* Trim trailing spaces */
    for (i = strlen (line.chars) - 1; i >= 0;
                            line.chars[i--] = '\0')
        if (!isspace(line.chars[i]))
            break;

    /* Check if this line is a blank line */
    if (!strlen (line.chars))
        stats[BLANK_LINES].value++;

    /* Do semantic checking of comments, constants,
       identifiers, and preprocessor directives. */
    parse_line (state);

    /* Trim trailing spaces again, since line is changed
          if comments have been deleted */
    for (i = strlen (line.chars) - 1; i >= 0;
                            line.chars[i--] = '\0')
        if (!isspace(line.chars[i]))
            break;

    /* Collect some statistics */
    stats[TOTAL_CHARS].value += strlen (line.chars) + 1;
    for (i = 0; line.chars[i] == ' '; i++)
        stats[INDENT_SPACES].value++;
    while (line.chars[i])
        if (line.chars[i++] == ' ')
            stats[EMBEDDED_SPACES].value++;
        else
            stats[NONBLANK_CHARS].value++;
}


/* This routine is called once for each file
   listed on the command line */
static void
process_file (fp)
FILE *fp;
{
    int c;
    struct _state state;

    /* Initialise global variables */
    state.in_num_const = state.in_string_const =
        state.in_identifier = state.in_char_const =
        state.in_comment = state.in_include =
        state.in_define = state.in_struct_dec =
        line.index = identifier.index = 0;
    for (c = 0; c < ELEMENTS_IN(stats); stats[c++].value = 0)
        ;
    free_identifiers ();
```

```
    /* Break file into lines, and process each line */
    while ((c = getc (fp)) != EOF) {
        if (add_char (&line, c) == '\n') {
            line.chars[--line.index] = '\0';
            process_line (&state);
            line.index = 0;
        }
    }
}


/* Calculate and display statistics */
static void
process_stats (file_name)
char *file_name;
{
#define SC(m,l,s,f,t,x)       { m., l., s., f., t., x, 0.0 }
    static struct {
        double max, lo, lotol, hitol, hi;
        char *name;
        double value;
    } scores[] = {

        /* max  lo lotol hitol hi         name        */
        SC(  9,  8, 12,  25,  30, "  characters per line "),
        SC( 12,  8, 15,  25,  35, "% comment lines       "),
        SC( 12,  6, 22,  46,  58, "% indentation         "),
        SC( 11,  8, 15,  30,  35, "% blank lines         "),
        SC(  8,  1,  4,  10,  12, "  spaces per line      "),
        SC( 15,  4, 10,  25,  35, "  module length        "),
        SC(  6,  2,  9,  17,  23, "  reserved words       "),
        SC( 14,  4,  5,  10,  14, "  identifier length    "),
        SC(-20,  1,  3, 199, 200, "  gotos                "),
        SC(  5,  0,  3,   3,   4, "  include files        "),
        SC(  8,  8, 12,  20,  24, "% defines             ")
    };
    int i, sl;
    double nc_lines;        /* Number of non-comment lines */
    double nc_nb_lines;     /* Number of non-comment
                                        non-blank lines */
    double score, total_score;
    struct _user_ident *ui = first_user_ident;

    nc_lines = stats[TOTAL_LINES].value
                        - stats[COMMENT_LINES].value;
    nc_nb_lines = nc_lines - stats[BLANK_LINES].value;

    /* Calculate the reserved words variety statistic */
    for (i = 0; i < ELEMENTS_IN(reserved_words); i++)
        if (reserved_words[i].used)
            stats[RESWORD_VARIETY].value++;

    /* Print out statistics gathered */
    printf ("%s:\n\n", file_name);

    for (i = 0; i < ELEMENTS_IN(stats); i++)
        printf ("%s %10d\n", stats[i].title, stats[i].value);
    printf ("\n\n");

    /* Calculate derived statistics */
    scores[0].value = RDIV(stats[NONBLANK_CHARS].value,
                            nc_nb_lines);
    scores[1].value = 100 * RDIV(stats[COMMENT_LINES].value,
                            stats[TOTAL_LINES].value);
    scores[2].value = 100 * RDIV(stats[INDENT_SPACES].value,
                            stats[TOTAL_CHARS].value);
    scores[3].value = 100 * RDIV(stats[BLANK_LINES].value,
```

```
                                    nc_lines);
    scores[4].value = RDIV(stats[EMBEDDED_SPACES].value,
                            nc_nb_lines);
    scores[5].value = RDIV(nc_nb_lines,
                            stats[MODULES].value);
    scores[6].value = stats[RESWORD_VARIETY].value;

    /* Calculate the average user identifier length */
    for (sl = i = 0; ui; i++, ui = ui->next)
        sl += strlen (ui->name);
    scores[7].value = RDIV(sl, i);

    scores[8].value = stats[GOTOS].value;
    scores[9].value = stats[INCLUDE_LINES].value;
    scores[10].value = 100 *
                        RDIV(stats[DEFINE_LINES].value, i);

    /* Calculate and print individual scores
       and add 'em up. */
    total_score = 0.0;
    for (i = 0; i < 11; i++) {
        score = 0.0;

        /* Use maximum score if value in ideal range */
        if (scores[i].value >= scores[i].lotol &&
                scores[i].value <= scores[i].hitol)
            score = scores[i].max;

        /* Otherwise interpolate to get score */
        else if (scores[i].value >= scores[i].lo &&
                scores[i].value < scores[i].lotol)
            score = scores[i].max * RDIV(scores[i].value -
                scores[i].lo, scores[i].lotol -
                scores[i].lo);
        else if (scores[i].value > scores[i].hitol &&
                scores[i].value <= scores[i].hi)
            score = scores[i].max * RDIV(scores[i].hi -
                scores[i].value, scores[i].hi -
                scores[i].hitol);

        printf ("%5.1f%s : %5.1f   (max %3.0f)\n",
                scores[i].value, scores[i].name,
                score, scores[i].max);
        total_score += score;
    }
    printf ("\nScore (%s): %5.1f\n\n\n",
            file_name, total_score);
}


/* Perform style analysis on each file on the command line */
main (argc, argv)
int argc;
char *argv[];
{
    int argv_index;
    FILE *fp;

    /* First, initialise space for identifiers
       and input line */
    if ((identifier.chars =
            malloc (identifier.size = 128)) == NULL ||
            (line.chars = malloc (line.size = 128)) == NULL) {
        fprintf (stderr, "Error allocating 256 bytes.\n");
        exit (1);
    }
```

```
    /* Process each file, and print its statistics */
    for (argv_index = 1; argv_index < argc; argv_index++) {
        if ((fp = fopen (argv[argv_index], "r")) == NULL) {
            perror (argv[argv_index]);
            continue;
        }
        process_file (fp);
        fclose (fp);
        process_stats (argv[argv_index]);
    }
    return 0;
}


/* Check if str is a reserved word */
static
is_reserved (str, state)
char *str;
struct _state *state;
{
    int i;

    /* Look through the reserved words table for a match */
    for (i = 0; i < ELEMENTS_IN(reserved_words); i++)
        if (!strcmp (str, reserved_words[i].identifier))
            break;

    /* Return zero if not found in table */
    if (i >= ELEMENTS_IN(reserved_words))
        return 0;

    /* Mark reserved word as used and check for goto's
       and global structure declarations */
    reserved_words[i].used = 1;
    if (!strcmp (str, "goto"))
        stats[GOTOS].value++;
    if (level == 0 && (!strcmp (str, "union") ||
                       !strcmp (str, "struct")))
        state->in_struct_dec = 1;

    return 1;
}


/* Scan through a string or character constant */
static
parse_const (delimiter)
char delimiter;          /* Constant type: (") for string,
                            (') for character */
{
    for ( ; *lineptr; lineptr++)

        /* Be certain to skip characters quoted
           with a backslash */
        if (*lineptr == '\\' && *(lineptr + 1))
            *++lineptr = '.';

        else if (*lineptr == delimiter)

            /* Found end of constant */
            return 0;
        else if (*lineptr == ' ')

            /* Make sure quoted spaces are not
               counted as embedded */
            *lineptr = '.';
    return 1;
}
```

```
/* Parse a reserved word or user identifer */
static
parse_ident (state)
struct _state *state;
{
    /* Collect characters into identifier buffer */
    while (*lineptr && (isalnum(*lineptr) ||
                            *lineptr == '_'))
        (void) add_char (&identifier, *lineptr++);

    /* Check if identifier is continued on next line */
    if (*lineptr == '\\' && *(lineptr + 1) == '\0')
        return 1;

    /* Add trailing null */
    (void) add_char (&identifier, '\0');

    /* Backup so terminating character is
       next to be scanned */
    lineptr--;

    /* Check if reserved or a user identifier */
    if (!is_reserved (identifier.chars, state))
        add_identifier (identifier.chars);

    identifier.index = 0;
    return 0;
}


/* Parse numeric constant */
static
parse_num_const ()
{
    /* Skip through leading numbers, letters, and dots. */
    while (*++lineptr && (isalnum(*lineptr) ||
            *lineptr == '.'))
        ;

    /* Check for exponent */
    if (*lineptr && (*lineptr == '+' ||
            *lineptr == '-') &&
            *++lineptr && isdigit(*lineptr))
        while (*++lineptr && isalnum(*lineptr))
            ;

    /* Check if continued on next line */
    if (*lineptr == '\\' && *(lineptr + 1) == '\0')
        return 1;

    /* Backup so terminating character
       is next to be scanned */
    lineptr--;
    return 0;
}

[ style 79.8 ]
```

## THE OUTPUT

```
style.c:

Blank lines              111
Total lines              728
Total characters       15932
Indented spaces         3166
Embedded spaces         1283
Nonblank characters    10755
Comment lines            141
Include lines              2
Define lines              21
Modules                   14
Goto's                     0
Reserved word variety     16
Non-reserved words       131


22.6   characters per line  :    9.0   (max    9)
19.4%  comment lines        :   12.0   (max   12)
19.9%  indentation          :   10.4   (max   12)
18.9%  blank lines          :   11.0   (max   11)
 2.7   spaces per line      :    4.5   (max    8)
34.0   module length        :    1.5   (max   15)
16.0   reserved words       :    6.0   (max    6)
 6.9   identifier length    :   14.0   (max   14)
 0.0   gotos                :    0.0   (max  -20)
 2.0   include files        :    3.3   (max    5)
16.0%  defines              :    8.0   (max    8)

Score (style.c):  79.8
```

# Appendix 2: Tabulated and Listed Information

## Alphabetic List of Keywords

| | |
|---|---|
| auto | storage class specifier |
| break | statement |
| case | statement prefix within a switch statement |
| char | type specifier |
| const | storage class specifier |
| continue | statement |
| default | statement prefix within a switch statement |
| do | statement |
| double | type specifier |
| else | statement |
| enum | type specifier |
| extern | storage class specifier |
| float | type specifier |
| for | statement |
| goto | statement |
| if | statement |
| int | type specifier |
| long | type specifier |
| register | storage class specifier |
| return | statement |
| short | storage class specifier |
| signed | type specifier |
| sizeof | unary operator |
| static | storage class specifier |
| struct | type specifier |
| switch | statement |
| typedef | storage class specifier |
| union | type specifier |
| unsigned | type specifier |
| void | type specifier |
| volatile | storage class specifier |
| while | statement |

Use of any of the keywords as identifiers will cause syntax errors. The ease with which such errors can be related to the source of the problem will depend on the particular implementation of C.

In addition to the above keywords, the C standard defines reserved identifiers. If any of the reserved names are redefined by the program, the behaviour is undefined and the program is thus not portable. The standard defines the following reserved identifiers:

- any macro name defined in the header files described in Chapter 12, if the corresponding header file is included;

- any identifier described in Chapter 12 and having an external linkage;

- any identifier described in Chapter 12, with file scope, if the corresponding header file is included;

- any identifier which begins with an underscore and an upper case letter or another underscore;

- any identifier which begins with an underscore (reserved for use as an identifier with file scope).

## C Operator Precedence

In the following table, C operators are grouped by precedence in the evaluation order. Operators within the same group have equal precedence. The associativity rule governs the grouping of expression with operators of equal precedence.

| Group | Operator | Description | Associativity |
|---|---|---|---|
| Postfix | () | Function call | Left to Right |
| | [] | Array subscript | |
| | → | Indirect component selector | |
| | . | Direct component selector | |
| Unary | ! | Logical negation (NOT) | Right to Left |
| | ~ | Bitwise (1's) complement | |
| | + | Unary plus | |
| | - | Unary minus | |
| | ++ | Preincrement or postincrement | |
| | -- | Predecrement or postdecrement | |
| | & | Address | |
| | * | Indirection | |

| | sizeof | Size of operand in bytes | |
| --- | --- | --- | --- |
| | (type) | Cast | |
| Multiplicative | * | Multiply | Left to Right |
| | / | Divide | |
| | % | Remainder (modulus) | |
| Additive | + | Binary plus | Left to Right |
| | − | Binary minus | |
| Shift | << | Shift left | Left to Right |
| | << | Shift right | |
| Relational | < | Less than | Left to Right |
| | <= | Less than or equal to | |
| | > | Greater than | |
| | >= | Greater than or equal to | |
| Equality | == | Equal to | Left to Right |
| | != | Not equal to | |
| And | & | Bitwise AND | Left to Right |
| Xor | ^ | Bitwise XOR | Left to Right |
| Or | \| | Bitwise OR | Left to Right |
| Logical and | && | Logical AND | Left to Right |
| Logical or | \|\| | Logical OR | Left to Right |
| Conditional | ?: | if a then x, else y | Right to Left |
| Assignment | = | Simple assignment | Right to Left |
| | *= | Assign product | |
| | /= | Assign quotient | |
| | %= | Assign modulus | |
| | += | Assign sum | |
| | -= | Assign difference | |
| | &= | Assign bitwise AND | |
| | ^= | Assign bitwise XOR | |
| | \|= | Assign bitwise OR | |
| | <<= | Assign left shifted | |
| | >>= | Assign right shifted | |
| Comma | | Evaluate | Left to Right |

# C Basic Data Types

char
: A character variable can hold any character from the basic character set represented as an appropriate integer character code.

signed
: There are four signed integer types: *signed char, short int, int* and *long int*. The list describes integer types of increasing range of values. *signed char* occupies the same amount of storage as a normal *char*. *int* has a size suggested by the architecture of the underlying hardware and can contain any value between *INT_MIN* and *INT_MAX* as defined in *<limits.h>*

unsigned
: For each of the signed types there is a corresponding unsigned type which uses the same amount of storage. The range of non-negative values of a signed type is a subrange of the values of the corresponding unsigned type and the standard guarantees that the representation of the same value in each corresponding type is the same. *<limits.h>* defines the ranges of possible values.

float
: A subset of floating point values representable by *double* can be represented by this type.

double
: A subset of floating point values representable by *long double* can be represented by this type.

long double
: A maximum possible range of floating point values (implementation dependent) can be represented by variables of this type.

enum
: A variable of this type consists of a set of named integer constant values and can be represented by the integer types.

void
: An empty set of values. This type is incomplete and can never be completed.

More complex data types can be constructed from the above set by recursively applying the following methods:

array
: A contiguous, nonempty set of values of a specific type.

structure
: A sequential, nonempty set of member objects.

union
: An overlapping, nonempty set of member objects.

function
: A function characterised by its return type and the number and types of its arguments.

pointer      An object whose value provides a reference to an object of a specified type.

## Escape Characters

The backslash character is used to construct escape sequences, that is, it is used to represent certain non-printing characters by a pair of characters, the first of which is the backslash. The following characters can be represented in this way:

| Sequence | Value | Description |
|---|---|---|
| \a | 0x07 | alarm (bell) |
| \b | 0x08 | backspace |
| \f | 0x0c | formfeed |
| \n | 0x0a | newline |
| \r | 0x0d | carriage return |
| \t | 0x09 | horizontal tab |
| \v | 0x0b | vertical tab |
| \\ | 0x5c | backslash |
| \' | 0x27 | apostrophe |
| \" | 0x22 | quote (inside strings) |
| \? | 0x3f | question mark |

In addition, any character can be represented by the corresponding integer code in its octal or hexadecimal representation as follows: \ooo where *ooo* is a string of up to three octal digits, or \xhh where *hh* is a string of up to two hexadecimal digits. For example: \10 is equivalent to \b, the backspace character, and \x20 is the space character.

Escape sequences such as those illustrated above may be used in strings, particularly format control strings:

```
printf ("\t result = \n");
```
and as character constants:

```
bell = '\a';
```

## Conversion Characters in Format Strings

The following conversion characters can be used in format strings controlling input and output. Full description of the input and output functions is given in chapter 3. Examples of the use of the control strings may be found in tables 3.1 and 3.2.

Modifiers:

| printf | scanf | Description |
|--------|-------|-------------|
| h | h | short for d, o, u, x, X |
| l | l | long for d, o, u, x, X |
|   |   | double for e, E, f, g, G |
| L | L | long for d, o, u, x, X |
|   |   | long double for e, E, f, g, G |

Type:

| printf | scanf | Description |
|--------|-------|-------------|
| c | c | single character |
| d | d | signed decimal int |
|   | D | signed long decimal int |
| o | o | unsigned octal int |
|   | O | unsigned long octal int |
| u | u | unsigned decimal int |
|   | U | unsigned long decimal int |
| x | x | unsigned hexadecimal int |
|   | X | unsigned long hexadecimal int |
| f | f | floating point [-]dddd.ddd |
| e | e | floating point [-]d.ddd e [+/-]ddd |
| g | g | format e or f based on precision |
| s | s | character string |
| % | % | the % character |
| n | n | count of characters processed so far |

Any invalid conversion character is printed.

# ASCII Character Set

ASCII Character Codes

| DEC | OCT | HEX | CHAR | DEC | OCT | HEX | CHAR |
|-----|-----|-----|------|-----|-----|-----|------|
| 0 | 000 | 00 | ^@ | 32 | 040 | 20 | |
| 1 | 001 | 01 | ^A | 33 | 041 | 21 | ! |
| 2 | 002 | 02 | ^B | 34 | 042 | 22 | " |
| 3 | 003 | 03 | ^C | 35 | 043 | 23 | # |
| 4 | 004 | 04 | ^D | 36 | 044 | 24 | $ |
| 5 | 005 | 05 | ^E | 37 | 045 | 25 | % |
| 6 | 006 | 06 | ^F | 38 | 046 | 26 | & |
| 7 | 007 | 07 | ^G | 39 | 047 | 27 | ' |
| 8 | 010 | 08 | ^H | 40 | 050 | 28 | ( |
| 9 | 011 | 09 | ^I | 41 | 051 | 29 | ) |
| 10 | 012 | 0a | ^J | 42 | 052 | 2a | * |
| 11 | 013 | 0b | ^K | 43 | 053 | 2b | + |
| 12 | 014 | 0c | ^L | 44 | 054 | 2c | , |
| 13 | 015 | 0d | ^M | 45 | 055 | 2d | - |
| 14 | 016 | 0e | ^N | 46 | 056 | 2e | . |
| 15 | 017 | 0f | ^O | 47 | 057 | 2f | / |
| 16 | 020 | 1 | ^P | 48 | 060 | 30 | 0 |
| 17 | 021 | 11 | ^Q | 49 | 061 | 31 | 1 |
| 18 | 022 | 12 | ^R | 50 | 062 | 32 | 2 |
| 19 | 023 | 13 | ^S | 51 | 063 | 33 | 3 |
| 20 | 024 | 14 | ^T | 52 | 064 | 34 | 4 |
| 21 | 025 | 15 | ^U | 53 | 065 | 35 | 5 |
| 22 | 026 | 16 | ^V | 54 | 066 | 36 | 6 |
| 23 | 027 | 17 | ^W | 55 | 067 | 37 | 7 |
| 24 | 030 | 18 | ^X | 56 | 070 | 38 | 8 |
| 25 | 031 | 19 | ^Y | 57 | 071 | 39 | 9 |
| 26 | 032 | 1a | ^Z | 58 | 072 | 3a | : |
| 27 | 033 | 1b | ^[ | 59 | 073 | 3b | ; |
| 28 | 034 | 1c | ^\ | 60 | 074 | 3c | < |
| 29 | 035 | 1d | ^] | 61 | 075 | 3d | = |
| 30 | 036 | 1e | ^^ | 62 | 076 | 3e | > |
| 31 | 037 | 1f | ^_ | 63 | 077 | 3f | ? |

ASCII Character Codes

| DEC | OCT | HEX | CHAR | DEC | OCT | HEX | CHAR |
|-----|-----|-----|------|-----|-----|-----|------|
| 64 | 100 | 40 | @ | 96 | 140 | 60 | ` |
| 65 | 101 | 41 | A | 97 | 141 | 61 | a |
| 66 | 102 | 42 | B | 98 | 142 | 62 | b |
| 67 | 103 | 43 | C | 99 | 143 | 63 | c |
| 68 | 104 | 44 | D | 100 | 144 | 64 | d |
| 69 | 105 | 45 | E | 101 | 145 | 65 | e |
| 70 | 106 | 46 | F | 102 | 146 | 66 | f |
| 71 | 107 | 47 | G | 103 | 147 | 67 | g |
| 72 | 110 | 48 | H | 104 | 150 | 68 | h |
| 73 | 111 | 49 | I | 105 | 151 | 69 | i |
| 74 | 112 | 4a | J | 106 | 152 | 6a | j |
| 75 | 113 | 4b | K | 107 | 153 | 6b | k |
| 76 | 114 | 4c | L | 108 | 154 | 6c | l |
| 77 | 115 | 4d | M | 109 | 155 | 6d | m |
| 78 | 116 | 4e | N | 110 | 156 | 6e | n |
| 79 | 117 | 4f | O | 111 | 157 | 6f | o |
| 80 | 120 | 50 | P | 112 | 160 | 70 | p |
| 81 | 121 | 51 | Q | 113 | 161 | 71 | q |
| 82 | 122 | 52 | R | 114 | 162 | 72 | r |
| 83 | 123 | 53 | S | 115 | 163 | 73 | s |
| 84 | 124 | 54 | T | 116 | 164 | 74 | t |
| 85 | 125 | 55 | U | 117 | 165 | 75 | u |
| 86 | 126 | 56 | V | 118 | 166 | 76 | v |
| 87 | 127 | 57 | W | 119 | 167 | 77 | w |
| 88 | 130 | 58 | X | 120 | 170 | 78 | x |
| 89 | 131 | 59 | Y | 121 | 171 | 79 | y |
| 90 | 132 | 5a | Z | 122 | 172 | 7a | z |
| 91 | 133 | 5b | [ | 123 | 173 | 7b | { |
| 92 | 134 | 5c | \ | 124 | 174 | 7c | \| |
| 93 | 135 | 5d | ] | 125 | 175 | 7d | } |
| 94 | 136 | 5e | ^ | 126 | 176 | 7e | ~ |
| 95 | 137 | 5f | _ | 127 | 177 | 7f | ^? |

# References

Berry, R.E. and Meekings, B.A.E. (1985). 'Style analysis of C programs', *Comm. ACM*, **28**, No. 1 (January).

Bourne, S.R. (1982). *The UNIX System*, Addison-Wesley, London.

Dahl, O-J., Dijkstra, E.W. and Hoare, C.A.R. (1972). *Structured Programming*, Academic Press, London.

Feuer, A.F. (1982). *The C Puzzle Book*, Prentice-Hall, Englewood Cliffs, New Jersey.

Hall, J. (1982). 'A microprogrammed P-CODE interpreter for the Data General Eclipse s/130 minicomputer', *Software Practice and Experience*, **12**.

Kernighan, B.W. and Plauger, P.J. (1976). *Software Tools*, Addison-Wesley, Reading, Massachusetts.

Kernighan, B.W. and Ritchie, D.M. (1978). *The C Programming Language*, Prentice-Hall, Englewood Cliffs, New Jersey.

Kernighan, B.W. and Ritchie, D.M. (1988). *The C Programming Language 2nd edition*, Prentice-Hall, Englewood Cliffs, New Jersey.

Knuth, D.E. (1973). *The Art of Computer Programming. Volume 3: Sorting and Searching*, Addison-Wesley, Reading, Massachusetts.

Lewis, T.G. (1975). *Distribution Sampling for Computer Simulation*, D.C. Heath and Co., Lexington, Massachusetts.

Meekings, B.A.E. (1978). 'Random Number Generator - Algorithm A-1', *Pascal News*, No. 12 (June).

Rees, M.J. (1982). 'Automatic assessment aids for Pascal programs' *ACM Sigplan Notices*, **17**, No. 10 (October).

Uspensky, J.V. and Heaslet, M.A. (1939). *Elementary Number Theory*, McGraw, New York.

Wirth, N. (1976). *Algorithms + Data Structures = Programs*, Prentice Hall, Englewood Cliffs, New Jersey.

# Glossary

**ANSI standard**
As used in this book, a specification of the syntax and semantics of computer programs written in the C programming language as described in American National Standards Institute, Inc., American National Standard X3.159-1989.

**ASCII**
American Standard Code for Information Interchange, specifying a mapping between a binary code and a corresponding printable or control character. For example, a binary code 1000001 (or decimal 65) corresponds to the letter 'A'. The original ASCII character set has been expanded by various vendors to include certain graphics symbols and special characters.

## UNIX
An operating system designed and developed by Dennis Ritchie and Ken Thompson at the AT&T Bell Laboratories between 1969 an 1971. The use of the system was originally limited to academic and research computer systems. Due to its elegance and power it is now in widespread use on a multitude of hardware platforms and supports a vast array of widely different applications.

**aggregate**
A collection of data of different types. Aggregate data types can be created in C by defining structures or unions.

**algorithm**
A problem solving method suitable for computer implementation. It is a set of transformations of inputs into outputs accomplishing a solution to the problem in a finite number of steps.

**application**
A piece of software implementing functionality required directly by the end users of a computing installation. The term is often contrasted with the *operating system* software.

**argument**
The actual value passed to a function at runtime when the function call is executed. All arguments in C are passed "by value", that is, a copy of the argument is made before passing it to a function. In order to access the original entity, not its copy, a pointer to that entity must be given as an argument.

**array**
A collection of data elements of the same type. Each element of the collection can be addressed by specifying one or more integer values called indices. An index is an offset from the beginning of the array in a particular dimension and in C always starts from 0.

**compiler**
A language translator typically accepting as input a higher level computer language such as C or Pascal, and producing a lower level output, usually in a language specific to the machine for which it was designed.

**constant**
A value which never changes during the lifetime of a program. In C, constants can be either literal, such as 42, 0x2a or "forty two", or specified by using the keyword *const*.

**declaration**
A specification of the type of a named object in a computer program. In C it is required that all data and functions be declared prior to their use.

**definition**
The actual specification of a function code. The code defines all aspects of a function, its parameters and behaviour, whereas a declaration (prototype) specifies only the type of parameters and the type of a return value.

**expression**
A series of operators and operands specified in accordance with the syntax rules of the language and producing a single value as its result.

**file**
From the perspective of a C program, a source for, or a destination of, data required or produced by the program. In that sense, a file may be the keyboard at which users type responses, or another program to which data are sent. One can also talk of physical files which are persistent representations of data stored on media such as magnetic or optical disks.

**function**
A sequence of statements which perform some computation. A well-designed function will have clearly defined inputs and outputs, usually passed via parameters, and should be free of side-effects - that is, no variables other than those represented by parameters will have their values changed as a result of invoking the function. A function in C is similar to a subroutine or function in Fortran, or a procedure or function in Pascal.

**header file**
If a program consists of more than one source file, it is usual to collect shared definitions in a separate file, included in all the source files. In that way, changes to those definitions are confined to a single file.

Definitions most often put in header files are:
    #include's
    #define's
    extern declarations of variables and functions
    typedef's of shared structures
Several standard headers are provided for C, which must be included in order to use functions from the standard library.

### identifier
The name used to refer to variables, constants, functions and derived data types or aggregates. In C, an identifier consists of a sequence of upper or lower case letters, digits, and underscores, and must begin with a letter. Although identifiers may be of any length, it is recommended that all identifiers are unique over the first 31 characters.

### interpreter
An interpreter accepts source code for a particular language and executes it directly. The difference between a compiler and an interpreter is that the compiler produces an object program, which is then executed; the interpreter executes the source program itself.

### library
A collection of common functions which may be used by a program if the library is linked with the program when the executable is built. It is usually provided in binary (and not source) format. In C, standard libraries exist to perform, for example, input and output, mathematical functions, and error and string handling.

### macro definition
Specifies a simple textual substitution of one character string in the program text by another. In C, macro definitions (or, simply, macros) may have arguments - although this may look like a function call, the macro expansion is done by the preprocessor prior to the compilation phase.

### macro processor
See preprocessor.

### operand
The object, typically a variable or constant, that is manipulated, or operated on, as part of an expression.

### operating system
Manages the resources of the computing environment, typically by providing file system maintenance, process management and other housekeeping functions. This represents the core, or kernel, of the operating system. A suite of other utilities are often provided for other functions, such as text editing and formatting, compilers and assemblers, and a command interpreter.

**operator**
Specifies the action to be performed on its operands. Operators in C are either unary, operating on a single operand (like the not operator), binary, taking two operands (like plus), or tertiary, with three operands (like the conditional operator).

**optimiser**
Code optimisation is usually performed as one stage of the compilation process. It involves, for example, moving operations whose operands do not change within a for-loop out of the loop, and eliminating redundant operations. Most C compilers offer this as a user-selectable feature at compile time.

**parameter**
A variable mentioned in the parenthesised list of a function definition or prototype. Contrast this with an argument, which is the value supplied when a function is called.

**pointer**
In C, a variable that contains the address of another variable. The value of the variable is obtained by dereferencing, using the * operator.

**preprocessor**
A program which performs macro expansion. For C, preprocessing occurs as the first stage of the compilation process. It is important to realize that most preprocessors are language independent - that is, C's preprocessor could equally well be used for some other language, since it is unaware of the specific syntax for C, and merely performs textual substitutions.

**processor**
The word 'processor' specifically refers to the CPU (central processing unit) of a computer, but in common parlance is used for the whole computer.

**program**
A set of statements that can be submitted as a unit to some computer system and used to direct the behaviour of that system.

**programming language**
A notation for the precise description of computer programs or algorithms in which the syntax and semantics are strictly defined.

**prototype**
An early version or example that serves as a model on which later stages can be based. Typically, a prototype does not implement all the features of a fully developed version. In C, a function prototype declares the arguments to a function, and their types, prior to its full definition.

**recursion**

The process of defining or expressing a function, procedure, or solution to a problem in terms of itself. Thus, a recursive subroutine calls itself.

**scope**

The time or region of a program in which the characteristics (e.g., type, value, etc.) of an identifier have meaning.

**signal**

An asynchronous event that arises in a program, such as a hardware or timer interrupt, or an error in program execution. If the underlying operating system supports it, signals can be generated under program control, blocked, ignored, or delivered to a function programmed to handle them.

**statement**

The unit from which a program is constructed; a program consists of a sequence of statements.

**storage (memory and disk)**

A device or medium that can retain data for subsequent retrieval.

**storage class**

The characteristic of a variable or identifier that determines the location and lifetime of the storage that represents it.

**string**

A one dimensional array of characters.

**structure**

A data type aggregate that is composed of smaller parts, which can themselves be aggregates. Each of the parts are individually represented by non-overlapping storage. At the lowest level, the parts consist of atomic data types, i.e., char, int, etc.

**union**

A data type aggregate that is composed of smaller parts, which can themselves be aggregates. Each of the parts are represented by overlapping storage. At the lowest level, the parts consist of atomic data types, i.e., char, int, etc. Thus, the same piece of storage can be interpreted differently according to differing data types in the union.

**variable**

An identifier used to denote a changeable value inside a computer or program.

**word size**

The length of a set of bits treated as a unit by the computer hardware. The number of bits in a word is typically a multiple of 8 bits or 1 byte. A word is usually long enough to contain an integer.

# Index